At Sister Anna's Feet

*An Old Nun and a Young Nun Break the
Holy Rule to Help the Poor*

Eileen O'Toole

iUniverse books may be ordered through booksellers or by contacting:

iUniverse
1663 Liberty Drive
Bloomington, IN 47403
www.iuniverse.com
1-800-Authors (1-800-288-4677)

ISBN: 978-1-4502-0456-9 (sc)
ISBN: 978-1-4502-0457-6 (hc)
ISBN: 978-1-4502-0455-2 (e)

Print information available on the last page.

iUniverse rev. date: 09/16/2015

For my husband, John,
and
my daughter, Elizabeth

SIS

There are people who enter your life and change you.
And then there are people who enter your life
and change everything....

Contents

Acknowledgments

I would like to thank my husband, John, and my daughter, Dr. Elizabeth Tegins, for the enormous patience they showed while I was writing this book.

I wish to thank Dr. Tom Quinn, now in heaven, and his wife, Rosemarie, for being my first friends after I left the convent. It was the two of them who suggested I put my stories into print.

For their encouragement and guidance, I thank Denis Hamill, Patricia Eisemann Logan, Andrew Blauner, and Hamilton Cain who all went out of their way to help me.

Mostly, I want to remember Sister Anna and Sister Muriel, who I believe are in heaven, and all the good priests, brothers, and nuns with whom I was privileged to share the work of extending God's love on earth.

Personal Statement

Spurred on by my Irish Catholic upbringing in the 1950s, I decided to enter the convent and become a nun at the young age of eighteen. Almost immediately I ran smack up against rules, regulations, and arcane practices that ran counter to my free-spirited nature. Deciding this life was not for me, I tried to escape, not once but three times in the first year. Each time I was found and brought back to live within the cloistered walls of the convent.

But in my third year in the novitiate, I was assigned to a mission where I would meet the person who would change my life forever. There, the elderly mother superior, Sister Anna, taught me how to develop my true spiritual self. She also showed me how to break the rules to assist those in need.

As the years passed, my work taking care of those who lived in the poverty-stricken Brooklyn neighborhood of my parish and beyond, brought me much joy and solidified my commitment to being a nun. However, all that would change when I received an obedience letter that reassigned me to a wealthy parish on Long Island. With that reassignment, the anchor that held me in the convent was ripped out from under me.

No longer allowed to attend to the poor, my life in the convent became unbearable. I knew the only way I could be true to myself and to the mission instilled in me by Sister Anna was to escape. The world outside would allow me to do what the cloistered world of a nun no longer would—tend to the needy.

But the decision was a lot easier than the deed. My family refused to help. With no one to turn to, I sneaked out of a spiritual retreat. I had nothing to my name except eighty dollars I had taken from the convent, along with my abiding faith in God. I was now in charge of my own life, but I had no money, no job, and no home. After seventeen years devoting my life to helping the poor, I was now, truly, one of them.

As William Cowper, the poet, states, "I was a stricken deer that left the herd."

It was Sister Anna's steely resolve mixed with patience and kindness that inspired me to take that fateful step out the door and down the road to the rest of my life.

Prologue

I sat behind the wheel of the convent station wagon, staring at the long road before me. I was exhausted from the stress of my problem. I was about to tell my sister, Margie, that I was doing the inconceivable—leaving the cloistered life of a nun and coming back out into the world to live. I would need her help.

From the main road I drove down several country lanes until her lovely home in Great River came into view. My little niece, Eileen, and my nephew, Michael, along with several neighborhood children, were playing outside, rolling down the front lawn.

I knew Margie was home, because her BMW was parked in the driveway. My heart began to beat faster at the thought of what I was about to put into motion. Suddenly the thought came to me that perhaps I should not do this. I can still feel the fear that filled my body at that moment.

The children came running over to the car as I parked it in the driveway. "Oh, hello, Aunt Eileen," they shouted excitedly. I got out of the car. My sister came to the side door of the house smiling and waved me in. She was eight months pregnant with Allison. *This is it*, I decided.

Over a cup of tea, I told Margie of my plan and explained as best I could how unhappy I was. I asked for her help. She didn't say anything for a long time. Then she got up and looked out the window. I could see that she was trying to digest everything I had just told her. We had always been close growing up, so I figured she and her husband, Pete, would naturally help me. I sat and waited for her response. When she turned from the window, I could see by the expression on her face that I was mistaken. She wore the same stern frown as when she reprimanded her children.

She took a deep breath and said, "Go back to the convent and do as they tell you. You must stay. I cannot help you. This is an awful thing that you are thinking of doing."

Outside, the sun was shining, but in this moment of time, I truly crashed into a most dark circle. Margie was very concerned about my parents. This act of mine would be the ultimate disappointment for them in their retirement years. Margie said she had to take the children to a game and left me in her house all alone. I cried and sobbed uncontrollably for a long time.

By four-thirty I pulled myself together, closed her front door behind me, and got into the convent car. It seemed to me that my life was to depend on what others wanted me to do. I could not understand why no one was going to help me.

Driving toward the highway, I knew that this less-traveled road was one that I must follow alone. My daily living in the convent was becoming a crucifixion with no resurrection in sight. I had to leave. It was painful to do—after all, I had selected this life. Where would I get the strength to leave it? After seventeen years, what could I do? Where could I go? I needed money, a place to live, clothes, and a job. Would I be able to do this? There was not one person in the entire world that I could turn to at this time.

All there was in my possession were a long black habit, black nun's shoes, and a shaven head. What in heaven's name was I to do?

The other nuns in the convent sensed what was up. Everyone around moved away when they saw me coming. It was considered a terrible deed to leave the order. I had promised sacred vows to God. Here I was, one of their popular, hardworking, creative nuns thinking of doing just that.

Very little energy was left in my body. I did not care that the other nuns treated me like a leper. Just as well. It was difficult enough to plan how I was to leave, and I did not wish to be pressed into conversation.

Sister Alma, the nun who had sponsored me, heard the rumors. She took the train from Brooklyn and a cab to see me. I was living and teaching in Our Lady of Lourdes in West Islip at the time. Upon her arrival at my convent, we went into the parlor and closed the door. Sister Alma said, "I think you should know that I have heard these horrible rumors about what you are thinking of doing. My advice to you is do not embarrass us by what you are about to do. Your family and I are very disappointed in you." Then amid this confusion, she called a cab and left.

After Sister Alma left, I heard the bell ring for afternoon prayers. I walked like a zombie into the small chapel of the convent and slid into my pew. I was one of the youngest nuns in the house, and we sat up in the front pew. I think it was planned so that we could not see the older nuns falling asleep. All during the chanting of the psalms, I was very upset. My body was weak, and all I could do was whisper the chants in Latin as I looked at the altar and then down to my prayer book.

When prayers were over, we bowed to the altar and walked in silence, heads down, arms inside sleeves, to the dining room in the main building. Since this was the time of Lent, we were not allowed to speak, which suited me fine. I could hardly look up or eat anything. I was steadily losing weight, and my body had become bone-thin.

After supper we went straight to night prayers and then to our rooms after offering up the Sacred Silence. I lay awake in my cell, knowing now that I would have no help from anyone. I had to be strong and plan my exit from the convent. I felt all alone in the world. Sleep would not come. I got up and looked out at the dark night with the stars above, blinking at me. I was terrified thinking of what I was about to do.

1
Where It All Began—Ireland

The O'Toole family was a proud clan from Galway, Ireland. But the only wealth they knew was the one pair of shoes that each of the twelve children wore to Sunday Mass in the village of Clifden. Poverty and hunger were synonymous with being Irish when my father was a boy. And few of his countrymen imagined anything better than what they already struggled to have and keep.

Faith was interwoven in every aspect of their lives. That was all they had to hold onto. The English had taken over Ireland and destroyed the land. In spite of this bad history, the Irish people held tightly to their faith in God.

I remember a story that my father told me. Teaching religion was forbidden in the country. My father's teacher would take the class up the side of the mountain and instruct the students in the Catholic faith.

There was a school inspector who would ride around on his motorbike to make sure the rule was observed. The teacher put my father at a site on the mountainside where my father could hear the motorbike coming.

My father would then run back and warn the teacher, and she stopped teaching about God.

The vitality of the church contributed to a relative stability in the family. Ireland had a thriving missionary movement that sent clergy and religious nuns and brothers to various parts of the world. In fact, every family wished that one of their sons would become a priest. It was considered a great honor.

This religion from the old country was practiced in our family even after moving to America. In fact, my father's sister, Tessie, became a nun in America to help the poor. She belonged to a missionary order of the Franciscans. In my own family, there were no boys, and though my parents were sad to see me join the convent, I knew deep down that they were very proud to have a daughter dedicate her life to God.

Luckily for me, however, my father set his sights higher, so to speak. It happened on a day like any other. He was walking into town, holding a rope with a slow-moving cow at the other end. He was hoping to return home to his mother with money gained from the sale. And then it happened.

First he heard it, unknown, loud, above his head but unseen at a distance. Growling and sputtering all at once. Now everyone's heads were raised and directed to the heavens, looking for something they could not see. And then, there it was ... but what was it? Silver, dark, shiny, hastily coming closer, sounding less unsure, coming closer to their heads, and then thundering by overhead.

That morning my father was among the scores of villagers in Clifden who witnessed the first nonstop transatlantic flight from Newfoundland to the Irish coast. The pilots were named Alcock and Brown. They circled the town twice. It was a Sunday and most people were in church, but they all heard the roar of the engines. The plane crash-landed outside of the town, on a bog. The airmen were unhurt and stepped out on Irish soil. It was 8:40 AM on Sunday, the 15th of June, 1919.

Historically this put Clifden on the map. But more importantly, my father had been there. I can only imagine what went on in his sixteen-year-old mind as he witnessed this tube of metal in the air, and then on the ground by the bog. I can only assume that it took him outside of his town, of his country, off his island, and sparked the courage and tenacity that would someday become the cornerstone of my family and an essential part of my own identity.

The Vickers Vimy flown by Alcock and Brown

Used with permission from Kathleen Villiers-Tuthill

2
The World Outside of Ireland

My father returned home with the money from the sale of the cow and the story of the plane. Within weeks he had concocted a plan with a few of his buddies, and he smuggled his Sunday shoes in his jacket. He had a job across the river taking care of a plot of land. He took some of the money he was saving and went to his mother to say good-bye. It had to be a normal good-bye, one that she would not question. He told her he would be back. But it was a lie, and he left.

Along the road to town, he met his little brother Joe, and looked him square in the eye, waving a finger. "You listen to Mom now, you hear me?" And his little brother knew that Frank had left, but he couldn't have known at such a young age that he, too, would never see his big brother again. However, my father did return one time for a visit and to give money to his sister, Catherine, so she herself could come to America in the following year. That was the way it was in those days. Each child would go to Australia or New York and get a job to make some money to bring the next sibling over. The children, in turn, were able to send money back home to help their parents.

3
London Getaway

My father walked to the center of town, which was really the center of their young lives at this point. There, under the canopy of the local vegetable stand, he met his two buddies, John Flaherty and Joe Heaney. They helped themselves to some forbidden fruit taken from the outdoor stand and ran off into the direction of the ticket office, which was located off the main road leading out of town.

The boys had planned this after Mass several Sundays ago. It was the rush of their excited youth that caused them not to be afraid. This rush took them into the ticket office to purchase tickets on the small rusty steamship that would take them into the town of London. The three of them were buddies, cousins, on their way to America where the streets of New York were paved in gold.

When they first hatched this plan to go to America, they knew they needed a sponsor who would vouch that they had a place to live and a job that would support them.

They had heard that a cousin, Mary McDonough, lived in Brooklyn, New York. Her family said she had a large brownstone on Garfield Place. They knew another cousin, Annie Fleming, also had a brownstone in Brooklyn on Garfield Place. They both resided in the same area now called "Park Slope" between Seventh and Eighth Avenue.

The boys had sent a letter by way of the Irish post office to Mary and Annie asking for their help. My father asked his sister, Delia to pay for his passage from London to New York. The three women had to go to the immigration office in New York where they informed the officials in charge of passage from Ireland to New York, that they would sponsor the three boys. The three lads would have a place to live and a job waiting for them. The jobs were in the grain shipping industry, where many young Irish men worked when they came to America. It consisted of shoveling wheat grain from the docks of the navy yard onto ships. It paid well.

They were on their way to America. The girls could look up the manifest of the ships leaving London and arriving in Ellis Island, in the port of New York. In that way they knew when to meet them. I have a copy of the manifest that states that, "Francis O'Toole—a laborer—speaking English—from Clifden, Ireland—passage paid by his sister, Delia, O'Toole, was in good health and had twenty-five dollars in his possession."

After several years of hard work shoveling grain, my father became one of New York's finest—a policeman.

4

Signing to Go to America

The walk up the gangplank of the small steamer was filled with excitement that they had never experienced before in their young lives. The plank itself represented their venture into a new world— "up and away." The plank had a lot of motion as they ascended it. Their youth, as we all have experienced, carried them safely up to the top. The hull of the small ship was where they sat and waited and watched in awe as the increasing sway of the ship took them out into the deep waters toward London. Silence took over as the beat of their hearts could be felt by all three.

Arriving in London, they walked down the plank and received directions to the office of immigration. As they entered the office, their emotions were stirred up to the highest level. There were many forms to be filled out and signatures to be signed. No one cared what it all meant, as long as the result was America. As was the custom, there was a three-day waiting period for the process to approve their departure. One of the lads knew a fellow in London who had a room, so they proceeded to walk to his address with the hopes they could spend the three nights there.

My father knew he needed a suit when he arrived on the sidewalks of New York. The streets held gold, and he wanted to be dressed for the occasion. As they walked along, he spotted a tailor shop and told his two buddies to wait. My father entered the shop and asked the tailor if he could make him a suit. The tailor said yes, and my father gave him the money that the tailor requested. He was then measured as the other two waited outside.

They slept on the floor of the friend's room, which was in a boardinghouse on a street not far from the center of town. The next day my father eagerly ran to the tailor's shop for his suit. Upon entering and asking for his suit, the tailor turned to my father with a face cold as stone and said, "Get out of here, kid, I never saw you before and you never gave me any money. Get out before I call the local bobbies."

My father was crushed and afraid that if he got into trouble with the law, he would never get his papers to go to America. With head bent low, he left the shop as tears fell down his cheeks. The reality of his journey was beginning to take hold.

5
My Mother in Ireland

In the town my father came from, just existing day to day was tough. The land was rocky, and no one could farm there. The family had one cow and some chickens. The fierce gales coming in from the North Atlantic would send you shivering to the nearest fireplace. The two-room stone fisherman's cottage was the only shelter from the weather. If you wanted food, fishing was the only way to exist. The men went out into the wild ocean across from the Aran Islands to bring food home for their families.

My father told me stories about his youth. The men would take a little rowboat called a currach, out on the rough waters to fish for their families. Several times, my father as a young boy went with the men to help. My father said that he was so scared, that he climbed into the boat and lay down on the floor in the front of the boat, and never got up until hours later, when they returned back to land with enough fish to feed several families.

The conditions where my mother grew up were a little bit better than in the small town of Clifden by the rough Atlantic. The Geraghty family resided inland in the middle of the County of Galway, away from the horrific climate off the ocean. They also resided in a little stone cottage, as was the way back then. It was all the folks had, and they made good use out of the rocks and stones that were on their land. However, living inland, they did not have to contend with the cruel ocean winds that really were ferocious at times.

Even to this day, as you stand at the edge of the town of Clifden on a cold winter day, you can feel the fierce wind blowing very hard against your face. You shake with the cold, but at least you are sheltered by the warm ski jackets and parkas of today. It still gets into your bones, and you look for a good place to get warm. Usually a good pub close by will do the trick.

Three years ago I visited my mother's childhood home in Lehenaugh, Castleblakney, Ballinisloe, County Galway. It was a stone cottage with three rooms and no heat or electricity. This was the way of living back then. I presumed, as I took a peek inside, that the first large room was the kitchen and sitting room, for it had a large fireplace where they cooked the food and kept warm. The windows were a good size. My cousin, Ann Liddy, told me the other two rooms were bedrooms. There was a time when all ten children lived in that home. The young parents were good people and made sure the rooms were snug for their young family. They worked hard on their farm to feed the family.

I have a picture of my mother's family when the children were young. I think the ages of the children were from about two to sixteen. They are all dressed properly for the taking of the picture. I wondered where the nice clothes came from. It seems the families passed the clothes down to other families as their children grew. There was a story about a "mourning outfit." One lady in the town kept the outfit and would give it out when there was a death. The person using it would wash it and return it to the owner. She would place it in a box until the next death when it was needed.

During the winter the children stayed warm near the fireplace. They attended school until the sixth grade, but it really was equal to our high school

My mother's family

education in the United States. My mother and father were educated and able to help us with our homework until the eighth grade. I remember my mom telling me she did not like school. She would leave the house in the morning, but instead of going to class, she ran over to the field of tall wheat. Her long blond hair blended in nicely, and no one could see her. It was here that she spent many days playing until her older sister found out and told her mother. That was the end of her days of glory in the sun.

It is amazing that my parents were so intelligent and excelled in anything they undertook. They had such hard lives. The people of Ireland had a lot to endure. As each child in the family got to the age of sixteen, the decision had to be made to send them to Australia or America for work. There was no work for them in Ireland. If they went, though they would miss the rest of their family, they could send money back to the parents. It seems everyone waited for the postman to come down the road with letters and packages from America. It was certainly a happy day, and you could see the families dancing in the road. They could buy food and start to build new houses. All the neighbors helped each other in the construction of the new homes.

When you travel in Ireland, most times you will see the old stone cottages, now in ruins but still standing. In front of the cottage is the lovely modern home that was built with the money that the children sent back to their parents.

Aunt Peg's new house in Galway, Ireland

To leave Ireland and one's family was a harsh decision but a necessary one. The incentive was the thought that they could help their families by going abroad to work. Irish people acknowledge that it was the children of the families who went abroad and sent money back that helped build up Ireland to be the way it is today. The young people who left laid the framework for a strong economy in Ireland. This little country had the fastest growing economy in all of Europe—at least until the financial downturn of 2009.

The plan for my mother, when she reached the age of seventeen, was to buy a ticket to go on a large ocean liner that sailed from Cork County in Ireland into the port of New York. There she would be met by her older sister, Mary. They had arranged that my mother would work as a maid for a well-to-do family on Park Avenue in New York City.

My mom went up the gangplank with some other young girls. There was one pretty girl named Delia O'Toole who befriended my mother. After all, my mom was only seventeen. They decided to get cots near each other. The Irish youth always traveled the cheapest way—down in steerage. It was a strenuous journey. My mother got very seasick, and after that trip she was always very afraid of water.

Delia went up to her brother, Frank. He had made a return trip back to Ireland—the last in his life—to visit his family with his sister, Delia. She told Frank about this lovely young girl who was so very seasick. Frank told Delia to bring her up to the top deck and she would feel better. That was how my father met my mother—on a British ship belonging to the Cunard Line and going to America.

6
Arriving in New York

Imagine for a minute life in Ireland on a poor farm, living in a stone cottage of about three rooms, with an outhouse, and all the sisters and brothers crowded together in that small home. Now switch to a scene of walking up a large, very large, gangplank and waving good-bye to your parents. The mother and father stood on the dock and waved with tears in their eyes. They had done this before for their two older daughters.

The large liner blew its' loud foghorns three times, and the ship moved slowly out of port. People were waving and crying at the same time. For all of these Irish immigrants, this ship was heading out into the Atlantic toward an unknown land. The Irish were a very strong people. My mother knew she had to do this to survive and help her parents. But it was so terribly difficult for her to see Ireland, her homeland, disappear in the distance.

She was headed to New York City. Her sister, Delia Teigue, met her with hugs and kisses and took her home to her place on Long Island. My mother stayed there for a few days, getting acquainted with many relatives and friends. She needed clothes and loved shopping in the large stores. After a few days, she found herself accompanied by her sister, saying hello to the doorman of a very majestic building on Park Avenue. What were her feelings? Certainly her legs were shaking. She was a shy young lady from a farm in Ireland.

The doorman ushered her up to the ninth floor by way of a special elevator that just went to that apartment. She entered into a very different world. This place was certainly spectacular to anyone, especially to a farm girl. There were nine bedrooms in all, with each having its' own bathroom. Talk about culture shock. The wealthy family fell in love with my mother and treated her very well. The family kept in touch with her until her death. I remember their children came to my mother's funeral.

The family had a lovely bedroom and living quarters for her, which was in the part of the house near the kitchen. This was known as the servant's quarters. Her job was to clean the rooms and wait on the table. There was another young Irish girl named Maeve who did the cooking for the family. This young one also had her own private bedroom. They became great friends and socialized together. A photo of my mother and her sisters appears on the next page.

My mom absorbed all she could learn from this wealthy family. She tried to raise us like they raised their children. We had to have the best clothes from the best stores, had to walk straight, and had to have very good manners. We even went to the same dentist they used. My mother was very strict, for she wanted us to achieve and be successful. My parents sent us to private schools, which was a hardship for them at that time.

Growing up, we had a nice apartment in a lovely building in Brooklyn. I remember around the first of every month, hearing the plan about how much money to set aside to send back to Ireland, to my father's parents and my mother's parents. With this money both families in Ireland were able to build nice homes for themselves. I have been there, and the houses are really pretty and furnished very nicely. My father's homestead overlooks the Atlantic Ocean, and

My mother and her three sisters

my mother's folks built a large home of about six bedrooms and bathrooms, with nice gardens around it.

After all their hard work to give us a fine education, my parents were devastated that I became a nun, assigned to work in the worst possible crime-ridden neighborhood in Brooklyn. They were very concerned about my safety.

7

The Calling

There are people who enter your life and change you. And then there are people who enter your life and change everything.

It would be hard to forget St. Joseph's High School in Brooklyn, New York, which stands like a sentinel post between my past and the transformation I went through during my high school years. My parents sent me to a high school that was to prepare me for the business world. In those days, the FBI, IBM, and the telephone company were popular places to work. The pay was good, and the benefits they offered were excellent. I felt good about myself at St. Joseph's. It was an all-girls' school. I remember how hard everyone worked in our classes, hoping to obtain a good position after graduation.

No one here knew me in this new school, which was in downtown Brooklyn. Back in my old neighborhood, everyone helped raise the child. It reminds me of, "It takes a village to raise a child." If I were hanging out on the corner, someone would alert my parents. It was not a good idea to have your daughter hang out with the crowd on the street. My mom would walk over to the corner and motion me to come home. Of course I did as I was told. The Topols owned the six-family building where we lived. Nana and Pop Topol lived on the top floor in the front. We lived in the apartment on the first floor in the back. Nana would sit by her window and watch the neighborhood kids playing. If Nana saw something that she did not like, she would call out to all of us to behave.

At St. Joseph's, I was finally free to be myself. The nuns ran the school, and we were certainly watched, but in a way that was different from the neighborhood. I found out if you behaved and followed the rules, the nuns would smile and trust you. Then they would leave you alone. I managed to be on my best behavior in school. I enjoyed the feeling of being liked. Everyone likes that feeling.

My grades in high school were very good. I was happy there and enjoyed all my classes. I worked very hard. On the first day in business management class, the nun teacher asked, "Well, class, will Miss O'Toole or Miss Lynch get the highest mark in this class this term?" After that, I was known as one of the smart ones, and proudly walked the halls and rode the elevators of the school's ten floors. This was my school, and the teachers liked me. My English teacher, Mrs. Flanagan, took a great interest in me when she realized I was a good writer. I excelled, to her happiness, and she called on me often. Other students looked to me for the correct answers.

Sister Alma was a young, pretty nun who taught me accounting. She was very popular with all the girls. Sister Alma and I became good friends. She was one of the people that I could go to with any questions or problems about the school. Yes, Eileen O'Toole had finally become important on her very own.

My teacher took forty students to the IBM building in New York City to compete in a typing contest. I won first place over several other city school contestants. The officials of the contest did not believe that I could really type that fast, so they made me retake the test. I typed even faster the second time around. My parents were very proud of their daughter. They purchased a new typewriter for my personal use.

Sister Alma and I had many conversations about life in general. I had these emotions rolling within me, and without hesitation, I confided my innermost feelings to her.

One Saturday, I asked Sister Alma for permission to visit her where she lived. The convent was down the block from the ten-story high school building. I already knew that the nuns had little in the way of earthly possessions, so before my visit, I bought a few small gifts, including perfumed bath powder and a set of pretty bath towels. Sister Alma was always very happy, and I knew she would love these gifts.

I rang the convent doorbell. You had to wait when you rang. The nun in charge of answering the door on that day had to adjust her veil and habit before coming to the door. She might have been on her knees scrubbing a floor and had her veil pinned back and her sleeves rolled up. Nuns were taught not to appear like normal persons. You had to have a supernatural flair about you. If a nun was seen with her habit pinned back and sleeves rolled up, it took away from her persona. She would not give the appearance of a spiritual being.

After about five minutes, the door opened. I was escorted into a very nice sitting parlor that had a lovely thick maroon rug, matching drapes, and upholstered chairs. There was a straight-back wooden chair for the nun. Nuns were never allowed to sit in soft chairs. This was a rule for life. Mortification of the body was the way of life for nuns.

Sister Alma arrived shortly and gave me a big hug. I really was starting to feel like she was my big sister. I finally was able to confide in her about my thoughts of what I wanted to do with my life. Sister Alma did not push or encourage me to become a nun. It was just the opposite. She suggested that I go out on dates and live a healthy social life, for I was only sixteen. Now I was mixed up. My parents did not allow me to date yet, and my father disapproved of my wearing makeup.

One day, Sister Margarita, who was in charge of the drama club, asked me to accept the lead part in the annual school play. I was completely surprised. "Eileen," she said, "we want you to take the lead in the play this year. Do you think you can handle it?"

That day after school, I slowly wound my way home. On this sunny, cold afternoon I wanted to savor the feelings of this new me for a few minutes, alone in the crisp air. I twirled along the sidewalk, flaring my plaid uniform skirt. I thought to myself that I was well liked by my classmates. I oftentimes entertained them with my jokes and humor. My teachers, both secular and religious, seemed to feel the same way. My school grades hovered near the top of the class. Again the question came into my head, *What shall I do with my life?*

With my senior year in school just around the corner, I mulled over the question again and again. *Does God want something special from me?* A bold, clear thought suddenly formed in my brain: I shall become a nun like my friend Sister Alma. Perhaps I could serve mankind in a far corner of the earth—like China, India, or Japan.

Most of my friends attended the same catholic school in those days. I did not know very many people who went to the local public school. The church had a strict rule in those years that all catholic children must go to a catholic school.

Two of my acquaintances who attended public school were the Asimov brothers. Their parents owned and operated the candy store on Windsor Place now known as Windsor Terrace. My family lived around the corner from the store on Sixteenth Street. I stopped in their shop every day to buy candy, papers, or magazines, as did most of the people in the neighborhood. Sometimes I would sit on one of the high cushioned stools at the long marble counter and enjoy an ice cream soda. Stan, Isaac, and I would talk. Later, Isaac became world famous for writing exciting science fiction books. He was my hero, and I would often watch him walk to the local subway entrance to go into New York City to find a publisher for his writings. He was rejected so often but never gave up. I felt sorry for him. I told that story to all of my students every year. I heard that years later Stan Asimov became a vice-president at *Newsday*, a widely-circulated newspaper on Long Island.

Now how had I gotten so passionate about helping others? Our family life revolved around the local Catholic parish church and school. We observed at a young age how my mother and father attended church and helped others. We also had discussions at the dinner table about the world around us. Sometimes my father would share his experiences as a policeman about people in need that he encountered in his work. I noticed my mother doing errands for elderly folks who were housebound. These people lived near us. She didn't brag to anyone about her service, but I knew because I went with her many times on her blessed walks.

My parents attended the school play and were very proud of me. The nuns congratulated them, and that made them even more proud of their second daughter. Sister Mary asked, "Maybe Eileen will become a nun?" Startled, my mother answered, "Never—girls who are going to become nuns are quiet." Sister Alma was standing there and said, "No way, we need all the merry ones we can get." On the way home in our car, my parents eyed me suspiciously but said nothing.

The next few weeks were terribly confusing for me, as I played my future over and over in my mind. I dreamed of a range of careers, from FBI agent to a fashion model. My three cousins, the O'Briens, were working for the FBI. They were the children of Catherine and Paddy O'Brien, named Agnes, Rita, and Kathleen. Their home was also in Park Slope. I overheard my father telling my mother that he wanted me to work there with them.

8
Fighting It

I changed my mind about becoming a nun soon after graduating from St. Joseph's. The sisters were very disappointed when I took an accounting job at Merchants Fire Assurance Company on Maiden Lane in New York City. Since I was well trained for the business world, I was promoted within two months and received a nice raise. I met lovely people, both young and old.

This was a wonderfully happy time for me. It was quite a ride. After work all the young people would go out for the evening. The company was very social and held several large party functions during the year. In the summer we would go to a country club in Westchester. I still have the pictures of those times. Several young men my own age made those times very special. I loved the dating scene and watching others socialize. The city and its' nightlife were for me, so I forgot about the convent. My parents were pleased, for they thought this was a good choice—and I was making a nice salary.

I was stunned when the parish priest, Father Burke, a friend of my family, kept informing me of God's will for me. Sister Alma's letters expressed her ardent desire to see me. *Why don't they just leave me alone?* I frequently wondered. It was silly to think that I would pay attention to them now. I was not back in school. I surely had my eyes opened and shared so much laughter and fun that I wanted it to continue. My answer to both was to tell them about my interesting new career in the business world. I had money to buy what I wanted and was generous to my parents. I liked this way of living.

Eileen second from left end

The trees shed their leaves, heralding the arrival of winter. Father Burke dropped by my home with a stern injunction: "God ordained for you to follow through on the holy vocation given to people who are very special." I remembered the spirituality that I had wanted one year earlier. It was pragmatic and action oriented. Back then, I was going to help the poor, the oppressed, the homeless, and the immigrants, and also develop a harmony with the supernatural.

When I read the book *Celtic Christianity* by Timothy Joyce, a Benedictine monk of Irish descent, it reminded me of those moments in my life. He writes:

> *I believe it is very natural to look back at the faith we had as children, and consider it as normative, "what ought to be." We might remember a warmth, security, and*

protectiveness in our relation both to parents and to God.
Some feel they have lost their faith because they no longer
feel that way. Real faith development means change,
conversion, transformation. It means a deeper expression
of what our humanity is about so that it truly reflects the
image of God. This can be found only by going forward,
sometimes through darkness, always in faith and prayer.
The paradox then shines through, especially as we look at
some of our spiritual elders who have gone this way. They
do indeed manifest the simplicity, innocence, and security
of a child that comes from simple faith. But now this
faith has been proven and found worthy. The spiritual
journey requires work and commitment. The Celtic way
has shown how this might be done. (p. 159).

A week after New Year's, Sister Alma wrote and asked that I come down to her convent and see her. There I was on a Sunday afternoon in January, sitting in the same convent parlor as before. Sister Alma came in and greeted me. I was happy to see her, but not happy that they were putting this conflict in my life.

Sister Alma was a caring person. She sincerely was interested in me and happy to hear how well I was doing at work. My shyness at this point was evident to her. I knew what was coming. She understood. Nevertheless, she continued on in the same vein as Father Burke. True, she had something that I felt I needed for my own spiritual quest. Maybe I needed a lifestyle like hers—prayer and love and fun! Many others had taken this way of life. Should I try it? I left with the intention that I would meet with her and Father Burke in two weeks at the convent and we would settle the issue.

During the next two weeks, I thought, *What the heck, give it a try—I might like it.* When I shared this thought with my parents, they were not too happy. I now had a good-paying job and was working in the real world successfully. They told me I was responsible for this decision. "It will be a difficult life," they said. My father was very against it, and my mother figured I was too wild to stay. However, in keeping with the old Irish way, I knew that they would be honored to have one of their daughters become a religious nun.

Sister Alma became my sponsor. She was to show me the way. There was a fixed procedure to follow before I would be permitted to enter the convent. First, I had to fill out an application. Reverend Mother of the community would set up an appointment to meet with me down at their main college building. Sister Alma would accompany me. It was she and Father Burke who would vouch that I was "good material" for the sisterhood.

At the meeting, I was instructed to kneel at Reverend Mother's feet. Then she told me to rise and sit down. She had an old, stern Irish face. Her dark eyes peered into mine. "What do you want, my child?" she asked. I trembled and stammered my often-rehearsed reply. "I … I … wish to become a sister of your order, Reverend Mother." Truly, I could almost hear the angels sing and the bells ring. This was a great day for the world, I figured.

Next, she asked me numerous questions about myself. "Do you smoke, drink, have a boyfriend, date, and do you get along with your father?" The questions droned on and on. Much later, Reverend Mother told me to depart from the room and wait outside until she sent for me.

They had a meeting concerning my potential as a candidate. Time passed slowly. I sat alone in a tall stiff chair. The long dark hallway was plushly carpeted in dark green. Expensive artwork and Oriental rug hangings lined the walls of the hallway. I wanted to roam those halls, but I was afraid to move. I tucked peppermints into my mouth. Suppose they did not want me because I was too wild? How embarrassing would that be?

The big oak doors swung open again, and an old nun ushered me back into the large room. Somberly standing before me were Reverend Mother, Assistant Reverend Mother, the Mistress of Novices who was Sister Antonella, and my sponsor Sister Alma. Reverend Mother spoke. "My child, you may submit your papers. While they are being processed, you are to attend daily Mass, engage in no dating, and prepare yourself for entering the congregation by frequent daily prayer and sacrifice." Then she said that I could leave.

As she escorted me out, Sister Alma informed me that if all went well, I would be called back in about two months to see Reverend Mother again. During those months, my records would be thoroughly scrutinized. My life and that of my parents would be examined through the use of special clerical investigators trained to uncover anything that could potentially embarrass the order. Traditionally this order was the most sophisticated, affluent, and outstanding order of the church. It was of the utmost importance that they have candidates of fine "breeding" to ensure the good works would continue into the future.

If all the investigators gave me a clean bill, I would then be tested to evaluate my intelligence and vocational aptitude. Also, I had to have a vigorous physical examination. In a short time, they would be in touch with me.

The word spread through the neighborhood: "That girl is becoming a nun." Now boys would not approach me. The parish priest checked on my daily Mass attendance. Getting up in the morning was always tough for me and still is to this day. I wanted to forget my "vocation." Let me go back to my old happy self. Frankly, now it was too late to change my mind.

A boy that I knew had not heard about my decision, and he asked me on a date. It was to take a moonlight ride up the Hudson. We were with some other couples. All was fine, and we were having a fun time dancing and laughing. Then something happened. One of the other couples told him that I was going to be a nun. The fun ended. For the rest of the date, he treated me like the Blessed Mother.

The thought came to my mind often to enter the Maryknoll Order. That order sent you to foreign countries. Maybe it was there I was most needed. The Society of the Propagation of the Faith prepared a Lenten drive for children every year. Every child was expected to insert pennies into their own little cardboard box. This sacrifice was for the starving babies in China. In this way, the church emotionally manipulated children to help the missions. This is where I got the idea of going to a foreign country. After much soul-searching, I came to the conclusion that Brooklyn was where I would serve.

The letter finally arrived. It stated that my application was in order. If I successfully passed the exams, I would be admitted with a group of eighty-six young women entering on September 6. The letter further directed me to prepare to donate a dowry to the order upon the day of entrance.

During the nineteenth century, Catholic tradition had developed a notion that a nun, upon taking her vows to God, became a spiritual bride to Christ. The bride was expected to embark on her new life with a gift. My gift, my dowry, was two hundred dollars. This seemed like a lot of money in those days. My parents were sending my older sister through a Catholic nursing school, and my younger sister was attending a private Catholic high school. Besides that, my parents were helping to support their families back in Ireland. Bishop Boardman, a family friend, offered the money for this cause, claiming it was his privilege. My good mother would not hear of such a thing. "It would be just like you to leave the convent and waste the good bishop's money. No, we will pay for it and hope that you stay for a little while and get some credits toward your education."

When the test results arrived, they announced that I had passed with flying colors. I was now called to serve God and live a sequestered, holy life. There would be so many unknown challenges to face, but I felt that I could handle them. The Spirit of God, in my commitment to my fellow man, would assist me.

After these arduous months of preparation, I was ready to leave work in New York City and go on a two-week vacation to the Catskills, and then commence my new life. My friends approached my mother to give me a shower. A nun's shower was money gifts to help with all the expenses entering entailed. My mother again said no for the same reason—she thought I would be out in a year.

I had a very good time with my girlfriends in the Catskills. My sister Teresa went to the same resort the following year and met her husband, Tom, there. I thought the world of Tom and always felt I had a part to play in their meeting each other.

The time finally arrived for me to focus on entering the convent. Maybe I would survive and succeed, for I was tough and smart. I would pursue my passion for helping others, and at the same time, love life. The pieces of my life puzzle seemed to be coming together.

9
Receiving the Holy Habit

Why did I choose this order of nuns? They were the nuns who taught me in my elementary parish school at Holy Name, Brooklyn, New York, and in St. Joseph's High School. History tells us that the order began in France. The women were widows who offered themselves to the local bishop to be used to help in the problems that existed back then. Some of the nuns became involved in teaching, others in caring for orphans and the homeless, and others in taking care of the sick. They lived the life of nuns. Soon it became common practice for widows to become nuns.

What was this road that I had to travel to become a nun? I would enter the convent as a postulant for six months. During that time, I would be trained as a teacher, and I would learn the ways of the convent. After that, I was to enter a year called "The Canonical Year." It is at this point that you are taught to remove yourself from family and friends. You must partake in secular courses of study, and spiritual classes on how to pray and meditate. In two years, I would be allowed to take the first vows of poverty, chastity, and obedience. Poverty meant being detached from things. Chastity was to be attached to no one but God. And Obedience was the final renunciation to the bishop and Reverend Mother. The lessons we listened to directed that this life we followed would lead us to perfection.

What did an eighteen-year-old know about sex back then? Not much. The image given was a person hollowed out to be wholly filled with Jesus and God. As the days passed, I did not comprehend the vows and their meanings. It was like a sapling growing each day. You learned a small bit at a time. The vows promised to God before the sacred altar, on our knees before the bishop, would help us strive to be void of all self and all things, so we might be able to help others and not think about ourselves. We would be the willing channel of the spirit of God in the world.

I was now going to begin a new life of growing like a seed, to change and adapt myself to help others. It was poverty that was going to make me do without all things material, except for the necessities of life. Chastity would tell me not to think about my body as a sexual person. I had to discipline myself to put away all thoughts of a sexual nature. When I was eighteen, I knew little of what I was giving up. As the years went on and my body developed, I had much trouble keeping this vow, for I wanted love, attention, and family. My body responded to sexual scenes and thoughts, especially to some men that I encountered in my life. Obedience—this was a vow that Sister Anna would help me with. When you are young, you obey your parents. After entering the convent, it was a continuation—to obey our superior. When orders were given that seemed not to make any sense, we dealt with them in our own way as you will see in future chapters. So I looked forward and hoped for the best.

My trunk was packed. In it were all the clothes I would need for six years. The rules stated that we were to be supported by our families until final vows, at which time the community took over that responsibility. As I stated before, these final vows were for life. One could not leave after that time.

In the large trunk were sheets, blankets, three sets of clothes, underwear, two pairs of shoes, rainwear, and a heavy winter shawl. These items were on the list we were given when we were accepted into the community. Toiletries were also in the trunk. When we needed something replenished, it was our responsibility to ask our parents to mail it to us.

I did not purchase slippers. Instead, I bought a fashionable pair of black, flat Capezio shoes that were in style at the time. In my mind,

I thought that if I decided to leave, I would be able to walk out with these shoes, and not the big high black laced-up ones we had to wear. They would be good for running away.

The shopping spree to New York to select my things was unbelievable. At that time in my life, I was very skinny. The convent list instructed us to buy a high-laced orange corset, black cotton stockings, and high black shoes. It seemed there were at least five layers of clothing one had to put on under the habit or top dress. I was going to be a postulant, which is the first step to becoming a full-fledged nun. Postulants wore a long black dress. After six months, you became a novice in the full habit, but without vows. The veil was to cover your head. No hair was allowed to show, under threat of penance. It was called being vain. The plain outfit was suitable to forgetting about the young attractive body so as to dwell on the supernatural.

The day that I was to enter the convent was sad. My father did not want me to do "such a silly thing." My mother was convinced I'd be home very quickly. My younger cousins, James and John, who were like my brothers, lived upstairs with my Aunt Katie and Uncle Jack. They kept looking at me, not comprehending at all what I was about to do. I certainly did not realize what I was getting myself into either. My Aunt Katie and Uncle Jack moved away from me with tears in their eyes.

So before noon on September 6, my mother called to me, "Eileen, it's time to get dressed." I withdrew alone to my bedroom and looked at the postulant's outfit laid out on the bed. Reverend Mother was expecting all postulants to be at the novitiate building in a few hours. It would be a long ride out to the countryside. Unbeknownst to me at that time, the other eighty-six young women entering would soon become a very important part of my life. To this day, I remember each and every one of them. We went through sad, happy, and humorous times together.

I, Eileen O'Toole, age eighteen, was about to enter the convent for the rest of my life. As the bedroom door closed, I indulged myself in a long, last glimpse of my bedroom—the broad oak desk, the Oriental rug that graced the highly polished wooden floor, and my typewriter on a stand at the side of my bed. My phone was on the same table. Sunlight poured through two large windows. Beyond the glass panes, two large forest green awnings shaded the windows, which looked out onto a pretty flower garden that was cared for by the owners of the house, Nana and Pop Topol. They were like our grandparents.

The two of them went out in the garden nightly to water the flowers and check on their growth. They gave the flower garden tender loving care. If we went out there, we had to be very careful. There were brick walkways we could use to walk around and look at the different varieties of flowers.

Our lovely house was like the United Nations. We had the Polish couple, the Topols; their daughter and her family, the Babinskis; the Jewish family, the Edelsteins; our family and my aunt's family, who were Irish; and the young English couple, the Wogloms. Everyone got along. We were privileged to join each family when they celebrated their particular holy days and holidays.

Seven decorated dolls sprawled across my vast bed. The thought came to me that I would never again sleep in this bed, nor would I be allowed to come home for six years. My feelings roiled, confused. Suddenly I regretted my decision to serve God as a nun. I never meant to be a nun, for I was more tomboy than lady. Here I was, going to a convent where the gates would lock behind me forever. But I had my Capezio shoes with me. I could leave anytime.

Although troubled, I felt the excitement of a whole new venture before me. I knew my family would be extremely proud of me. In our neighborhood, any family that had a child in the religious life was looked up to as very special. It all seemed very profound: "Eileen O'Toole was going to help others in the world." This novitiate training period would be like going away to college. (Was I in for a big awakening!)

"Eileen, are you dressing?" called my mother. "We have a long ride, and you want to make a good impression on the nuns." "Yes, mom," I answered, strangling in my tears. My mother sensed my anguish. She strode into the room to help me dress. "Well, now," she said, "I left Ireland when I was seventeen, and I was very lonely, but we were never meant to be happy in this world. Since you have made up your mind and spent all this money, at least try it out for a while."

I knew deep down that my mother and father were quite upset over their second daughter leaving home. The previous year, my older sister Teresa had gone into a boarding school for nurses' training. They really missed her. We all did. While my mother chattered on, I began to feel God's will for me on earth was to follow his way and do the work he would assign me through others. But leaving home was such a difficult move. Tears welled up in my eyes.

Really, imagine me a nun! No one in the family or in my neighborhood could understand my desire to do such a thing. Teresa was the obvious candidate. She had wanted to become a nun for as long as I could remember. She faithfully attended Mass and Communion every morning, delighting all the nuns in the parish. Not me!

My younger sister Marjorie seemed to receive the lion's share of attention from the family, for she was the baby. She was also the prettiest and smartest one. Marjorie and I were good friends growing up, attending the same Catholic high school. She was very popular with the boys in the neighborhood, and I watched with envy.

My mother appeared at my bedroom door. She seemed very sad. I guess it reminded her of her own life, leaving Ireland at a young age. She knew how painful this was going to be for me. The postulant's dress was on the bed, and my mom helped me put it on. It consisted of a form-fitting dress that extended to the ankles. There was a short matching cape over the shoulders with a white collar. The long, loose sleeves were tight at the wrist, with white cuffs there to match the collar. If you remember Maria's dress in *The Sound of Music*, then you have a very good image of ours. It was, in fact, exactly the same style.

The convent permitted each postulant to bring two pairs of shoes with her. Poverty meant having only three outfits and two pairs of shoes. Our preparation for the vow of poverty that we would be taking in two years commenced on that day with the limited amount of earthly possessions that we were allowed to have. I was always very hard on shoes. After only a few months, my shoes were in terrible condition. Since the rule stipulated that parents had to repair the shoes, my parents would take the shoes home, supposedly to have new heels and soles put on them. However, those shoes were discarded, and my parents purchased a brand new pair of shoes for me. No one ever found out about this deal my mother and I had, but Sister Antonella would comment often on how Miss O'Toole's shoes were always nicely polished and how I took good care of my shoes, which showed that I cared for my vow of poverty. This continued for six years. The shoes we had to wear were quite expensive, but my parents were delighted to lavish me with this gift. Instead of feeling like a poor nun, I wished to be the "best-dressed nun" around.

For the winters, I needed a shawl. My mother knitted me two shawls. I liked to be warm, and Sister Alma urged me to purchase a piece of black flannel, 100 percent cashmere. I placed that between the two knitted shawls for added warmth.

The morning of the day I entered the convent

I recall one cold winter day that I was assigned bus duty. I often stood in the snow on a city corner for forty-five minutes in subfreezing temperatures. I had eight shawls heaped on me that day. The bus driver told me that he could not see me under the shawls.

All of my relatives were lingering in the living room. I was the center of attention as my bedroom door swung open and out I strode. This time, though, I didn't like it—butterflies were fluttering in my stomach. Father Burke sensed my fears. We posed for pictures.

Then, quickly, I was in the car, riding to Long Island and the motherhouse.

This was to be my home for the next two years. The drive was upsetting. I had to continue since I had planned all of this. I actually do not remember what we talked about during the drive there. My father was very quiet. I truly began to believe that day that I would stay in the convent for a short time and then head back home.

We drove through the large black iron gates, which were of great height and were quite imposing. On the other side of those gates was a long winding road, with very tall trees on both sides. We followed this road down to a vast and splendid line of adjacent buildings that housed the academy, the motherhouse, and the very impressive cathedral that was their chapel. Many other cars were there. The postulants were all arriving at the same time. My family and I got out of our car and walked up the steps leading to the door of the convent. There was a nun directing us to the inside parlors. The visiting parlors were on the first floor. It was a large, five-story-high convent.

10
The Not-So-Great Escape

Upon walking through the magnificent front doors, we saw how beautifully all the rooms were decorated. The chairs and couches were a matching soft velvet color of light rose. It matched the pretty drapes on the long windows. There were tables filled with plates of cookies, and they were serving coffee and soda to our families.

I met Sister Antonella that day. She was to be our Mistress of Postulants, meaning she was the "Boss Lady." It was her responsibility to train us to be future nuns. In our special outfits we were now known as postulants. It turned out that when I got to know Sister Antonella, she became my favorite nun. She was a very holy, grandmother-type person who appeared aristocratic with no show, in spite of her position. She never raised her voice, never got angry, and had a great sense of humor. Sister Antonella showed us a little of what God must be like. When I watched Pope Benedict XVI on his recent visit to New York, he reminded me of Sister Antonella. She looked into your eyes and could read your soul. I remember hearing the same thing about the pope. People who got up close to him said the pope looked at you directly and touched your soul.

The bell rang to signal that it was time for our parents and relatives to leave the building. I started to feel horrible and homesick. The nuns rushed us into the long marble hallway and down toward the main dining room so that we could meet the other postulants. I saw through a window that my father was hunched over the front of our car, crying. This scene was very hard for me to take. I loved my parents. What was I doing? That night I decided this would just be a visit to see what was going on inside the convent. Then I could leave. That made me feel better, and I followed the other postulants down the hall to the large dining room.

We ate dinner that night in the main building. It was here that we would have all of our meals. We were given assigned seats. After finishing supper, we were directed to the novitiate house. It was a little walk down the road. This house was the original building on the estate that was donated to the order by a wealthy family. The mansion was turned into the novitiate and divided into many rooms and baths for the postulants. We would sleep here, have classes here, and pray in our own little chapel. We were assigned roommates and shown to our rooms. My roommate was Mary Lou. She had long black hair down to her waist. We had so much fun together for a few weeks. Then she left. I was heartbroken.

The next morning after breakfast, we were assigned our individual tasks. They were called "charges." My first assignment, or "charge," was to clean and keep the large dining hall in the main building in order. I did this every day, three times a day, with two other postulants. We set up for meals, putting the food on big carriers and pushing them out into the large dining room. The dining room had about fifty long tables for eight hundred nuns. There were sixteen nuns to each long table. The tables were covered with fine linen tablecloths. Every nun had an assigned seat. At her place was a linen napkin rolled in her napkin holder with her name engraved on it. Usually your family gave this to you. I had a really nice sterling silver napkin ring that my parents gave me when I made final vows. This was one of the few items of value allowed to us.

A novice or postulant was assigned to each table to bring food, water, and whatever else might be needed. Reverend Mother and her assistants sat at the top end of the dining room, near the French doors and the gardens. Their table was on the dais. It was called table number one and was considered a place of honor. Then, in order of seniority, came the nuns who taught in the academy and nuns assigned to the main convent to perform various jobs. Lastly, at the very back of the hall, were the tables for the novitiate members. We were served last, and the food was not good. The best food went to the top tables. I survived on cornflakes three times a day.

Our charges were hard manual work, and we were not used to it. Every morning, I had to mop the center aisle of this magnificent hall. The floor was marble from Italy and was beautiful. The windows extended from ceiling to floor and were decorated with velvet drapes. The ceiling was very high, as you see sometimes in cathedrals.

When morning charges were finished, we walked back to the novitiate building in silence. By nine o'clock we were to be assembled, sitting at our individual desks, waiting for our classes in methods of teaching. Since we were to be teachers, this was a very important course of study. Following lunch, we had classes in spirituality. Then freedom came after three o'clock prayers. We were allowed to have milk and cake in the kitchen of the novitiate—in silence, of course. Talking was allowed after we finished. We went outside for fresh air and could roam the back lawn behind the novitiate for forty-five minutes. It was from this back lawn that I tried to run away three times.

The bell would ring for afternoon spiritual bible readings, followed by prayers in the chapel, and supper at six in the main building. After supper we were assigned to peel vegetables in the basement corridor. The convent had its own farm. We walked back to our building to prepare to study for our classes the next day. All of this was done in silence.

A bell would ring, at which time we went to the chapel to say night prayers and offer up the Sacred Silence for the night. This silence was not to be broken except for an emergency. Then it was up to our cells (rooms) to wash and get to bed, in thirty minutes. Lights had to be turned off when the night bell rang.

Kneeling on the hard wooden kneelers in the chapel was difficult. The prayers were long and in Latin. It never failed that one of the postulants would fall asleep and slide off the kneeler to the floor, making a loud racket. Of course, we all giggled. The nun in charge would come down the aisle and scowl at us.

Some of us had fun breaking the rules, as young people will do. We would talk, whisper to each other, and steal food to eat at recreation or bring it back to our rooms at night. Other girls were somber and would not bother with us.

Several times during recreation, I decided this was the day to leave. I would just walk toward the long road leading to the big black iron gates. The Capezio shoes were in my pockets. I walked as fast as I could the first time. Just as I neared the gates, a black limo with dark windows came up to me and told me to get inside. I did as I was told. I guess they were always watching us. I figured the next time, I would take a different route behind the building and run out the side gate. The next week, I suggested to three of my friends that we try it together. We walked slowly and calmly so as not to cause a distraction. Then, when we thought we were safe behind large trees, we ran as fast as we could, holding up our long skirts. We nearly got to the entrance and the gates. Again, the big black limo came and directed us back to the novitiate. I think they must have had guards on the path that alerted the boss nuns sitting in the convent. Nuns in charge never mentioned it to us, so we were thankful that we did not get a penance. Next time might prove successful, we said.

At the end of six months, we were formally received into the order. We marched down the aisle of the large cathedral chapel dressed as brides of Christ. The organ was playing, but it wasn't "Here Comes the Bride." I think it was "Holy, Holy, Holy." Our families were there. After praying at the altar, we went back to the dressing rooms in the basement, where we changed into the habit of the order. All the new nuns, dressed in their full attire, walked down the aisle of the cathedral in a procession. We professed death to the world as we knelt at the altar rail. There was a little reception. Then our guests left. I had told Sister Antonella before I walked down the aisle that this was not for me, but she reminded me that I was told to stay for a little while and not to bother upsetting my parents with my feelings. There was no doubt that I would leave shortly, with a few of my friends. So I just enjoyed the procession and the visiting with my family and the goodies we could eat.

My family on "getting the habit" day

The next day, we had our heads shaved clean! They brought us one by one into a private little office and told us to kneel down by Reverend Mother and bow our heads down. She had an electric razor and ran it over our heads as another nun held us down. I was in a state of shock. All my hair was gone, and my head was as clean-shaven as the palm of your hand.

We had to go out another door to go to our rooms, so no one in the front office would see us and learn what was behind that closed door. I ran up the stairs to my room and slammed the door shut. It fell off the hinges. It stayed like that all week as punishment, so I would have no privacy. I cried so much that they had to take my roommate and put her in another room. Every night when my head touched the pillow, the bristles on my head would scratch against the pillowcase whenever I moved. It was so devastating to have this happen to my lovely long blond hair.

The bell rang for us to assemble in the large classroom. This time I was going to be equally as shocked. We were told of "our mortification," which was to beat ourselves every Friday evening with chains that had thorns sticking out of the steel. This was to make up for all the sins that would be committed during the weekend by people in the world. Lights were turned off during this "mortification service." We were instructed to beat ourselves until blood came. I would not do it. I hit the back of the chair instead of my thigh. There was no way that we could leave at this point. Bald heads would be accepted today, but back then, we would have been looked on as freaks.

The training period lasted one year from that day. We were in cloister and were allowed no visitors, so we could not tell anyone what was happening to us. My bald head and the spiked metal chain for discipline were enough to tell myself that when I got out on a mission and could walk away, I would certainly do that. This was not for me! I would go through the canonical year, for I had no other choice. My friends and I helped each other through these very difficult days. "We can do this," we told each other.

On the bright side, I learned many lessons from that year. It made me a better person and enriched my spiritual life. I became not a self-centered person, but a person who found her true strengths and formed a generous, caring heart. Was it worth it? I cannot answer that question.

11
First Mission

After a year of intense study, tests, and preparation, we were deemed ready to be sent on a mission somewhere in Brooklyn or Long Island, where the community had schools. Our trunks were packed by us. We were instructed to leave the basement where the trunks were situated. We knew the sisters in charge were placing delivery labels on each trunk. That would tell us where we were going to be assigned on our first mission. Talk about excitement!

I tried to figure out a way to get to the basement, but they had all the doors locked. If they had caught me, I probably would not have been allowed to leave the motherhouse. They did keep some novices at the motherhouse. I think it was a form of discipline. After all, I was really looking forward to some freedom on a mission. If things did not go in a way that I liked, I could always put on my Capezio shoes. Leaving from the city would be real easy for me since I was a city girl.

The day before, the Mistress of Novices summoned all of us to a meeting in the lecture hall. Finally, after weeks of wondering and waiting and hoping, we were to learn our destiny for the coming year. Sister informed us that we were to be in perfect silence during the reading. I would describe it as being ready to hear our jail sentencing. The novices already out on the missions came back and related horrid stories about mean superiors in some of the mission houses.

My name was called. I was assigned to a school in Williamsburg to teach first grade. I had heard nothing bad about this mission. Here was where I learned how to teach and adjust to living in a small community of twelve nuns. I was the youngest in the convent and was not allowed to speak to anyone except these nuns. I stayed there from September through June, at which time I was to spend two months back at the motherhouse for more spiritual training.

St. Mary's in Williamsburg was not a wealthy parish. When they showed me to my bedroom, or cell, which was very large, I found that I was sharing it with two other nuns. My bed had three mattresses, one on top of the other. None of the mattresses were good, so the superior decided to stack them for me. It was a funny sight. I had to jump up every night to reach the top mattress, and I learned to slide off them in the morning when the bell rang at 5:15 AM to get up. A couple of times I had a good ride to the bottom, but then I got used to it.

The pastor of the parish was an old, weird man who did not like women. I remember he insisted that he was free to roam the convent whenever he wished. He also demanded that the lights be turned off at nine o'clock at night. If we went to the bathroom during the night, we had to use a flashlight or else he would call the superior and growl, "Turn that light off!" Thankfully I only stayed there for ten months. The superior was a very nice old lady. She had a bad heart problem. It was difficult for her. She was the principal of the school, and as soon as she came home from school, she had to retire to bed. I really liked her.

The thermostat was set at sixty-two degrees, and the pastor had a lock on it. It was located at the back of the chapel. One night we were all so very cold. I decided to put an end to this. Down I went to the chapel. My superior was in bed, so I did not have to tell her what I was doing. I tried so hard to unlock the thermostat box and change the setting. Uh-oh, I heard the footsteps of the pastor coming up the stairs. I quickly ran up to the altar and made believe that I was meditating before the tabernacle. My eyes were closed tight. He came down the aisle, and I felt him looking at me. Everyone was so relieved when he left.

I asked our kind superior why she allowed this to go on. She explained to me that she was sent there just to appease him. If he got upset with the nuns, he would close the convent, she would be moved as superior, and the children would have no school. I know now that I would have caused trouble for her if I had stayed longer in that place. Pastors were in complete control of their parish back then. Their personality determined the quality of life in the parish for the people, nuns, priests, and brothers. The same thing was true about the superior of the convent. She could be arrogant, or a model for sainthood.

The year went fast. I had ninety students in the first grade morning class, and ninety students in the afternoon class. The pastor wanted ninety in each class, so he could collect the most amount of tuition. There were twelve students who spoke no English, but they learned from the other children. Most of the students read at grade level by the end of the school year. We were well trained to be excellent teachers. I loved my students and we really enjoyed each other.

As I said before, my superior, Sister Mary, had to go up to bed directly after school due to her heart condition. The pastor seemed to delight in going up to her bedroom and bothering her. There she sat in her bed, with her flannel nightgown on (which was the rule) and a white head cap on her bald head. We all had to wear a head cap on our bald heads when we removed our veils. Also, we had to sleep with our arms folded across our chests. I often ask myself as I look back if the pastor got his kicks out of this.

The sad thing is that the two priests who lived with him in the rectory had to put up with so much. They were very unhappy in their lives because of this pastor. I remember one time a young priest came over to my classroom to talk about how miserable he was living in that rectory. What could I say? It took a lot of courage for him to talk to anyone, for he also took a vow of obedience to the local bishop. I was learning fast.

The young nuns in that house were very kind to me. Every night after night prayers they would sit with me and help me prepare my schoolwork for the following day. I did the same when my turn came to help young novices.

When June came, all the novices were summoned back to the novitiate for two months of religious study. We were allowed visiting once a month for two hours while on the mission. We were not allowed visitors during the summer months.

It was good to see our friends again and exchange stories about our experiences while out on the missions. We learned the names of the horrid superiors and listened to colorful stories about happenings on other missions. I knew there was a lot out there that we all had to learn.

I want to tell you about my dear friend, Sister Sara. She was a very happy, extroverted, pretty blond girl. We got along quite well. Sara and I were much alike. Sara frequently got caught breaking rules. I never got caught. Sara was always so happy that she did not even think of the consequences. She had a great personality. If Sara had stayed in the outside world, she might have been a Hollywood star.

After our two months of religious study at the novitiate, we were all assigned to new missions. I was assigned to a new mission convent house in Bedford-Stuyvesant. I hoped it would be a nice place.

12
At Sister Anna's Feet

The convent where my new assignment would be was called Nativity Parish, in the Bedford-Stuyvesant section of Brooklyn. I marveled at the Romanesque arches, large windows, and fine brickwork of this lovely convent that belonged to the parish. The block, which was populated by a number of storefront churches, was very nicely kept. However, go just outside this block, and you'd be entering dangerous territory.

My parents drove me to my new assignment. It was about three o'clock in the afternoon. They were instructed just to go to the front door with me and then leave. We rang the door bell. After awhile, the door opened, and the nun in charge of answering the doorbell that day appeared. In a cold, brusque voice, she said, "I'll bring you upstairs to see Sister Anna. Say good-bye to your parents." I kissed my mother and father and told them I would see them at the next month's visiting day. How sad it really was to see them turn around and get in the car and drive away.

The convent—the house for nuns—was a very nice three-story brick building, with a large backyard for the nuns. I could see that there was a big side yard for the use of the adjacent school. Our students were bused in from Flatbush. When the white parishioners moved away, they kept sending their donations to the pastor, provided that he educate only white children from the parish in Flatbush, which back then was a wealthy area.

The pastor had a school built for black children just one block away. They would not be coming to our school. It was called Saint Peter Claver School. "Peter Claver is a special patron of all the Catholic missions for the black people. During his life he baptized and instructed in the faith more than three hundred thousand black slaves who landed in the Caribbean" (Catholic *Encyclopedia:* St. Peter Claver).

We were friendly with the nuns from the Sisters of the Holy Family of Nazareth, a Polish order that ran Saint Peter Claver School. Not one of us liked this racist arrangement, but it was out of our control. The pastor was "king" back then. I was told just a few weeks ago, while doing research for this book, that the nuns in that convent heard of a black woman who went to Nativity for Mass and the pastor would not give her communion.

Saint Peter Claver School was a lovely building. The students cleaned the classrooms themselves after 3:00 PM when classes were over. I was amazed. However, some good came out of the bad, in that the students loved their beautiful school and were very proud of it. They worked hard in class and got great marks. It was a close family feeling that existed between the nuns and their students. The students in our school were bused back to their neighborhood after the dismissal bell rang. I often wonder what great successes came from Saint Peter Claver School.

Sister Anna was the mother superior I was to take care of. I dropped my bag and followed the nun up the stairs to the first landing. On the way to Sister Anna's bedroom, the nun explained where everything was. The first floor of the convent building consisted of a large kitchen, a pantry, and a very large, long dining room with French doors that opened out onto a private patio for the nuns. It reminded me of a Spanish-type portico. There were several rocking chairs scattered about the yard.

Sister Anna's rooms and a guest room and chapel were on the second floor, with a very large community room at the end of the hallway. This common room was so large that it was able to fit fifteen gigantic teacher's desks in it. The desks were placed around the room separate from each other. They were for the use of the nuns when they had spiritual reading and sewing time, and in the evening to prepare schoolwork for the next day. All of this work was to be done in silence. Also, nuns were never allowed to go from one room to another without asking permission of the senior nun to leave.

The third (top) floor had two wings. The older nuns lived in the front wing, which had twelve rooms. The hallway going to the back part had four bedrooms for the younger nuns. This was where I was assigned my room. It was about six feet by eight feet. Each room consisted of a single bed, small desk, lamp, chair, sink, and window. Bathrooms and shower rooms were down the hall between the wings.

As I reached the landing, I turned to my left and walked into Sister Anna's bedroom. The door was open, as I later learned it always was, because Sister liked to be a vibrant part of life in the convent. Inside the sun-filled room, sitting in a big, overstuffed leather chair, was a short, very heavy nun, her hands clasped together at her waist. This was my first inkling that Sister Anna was not

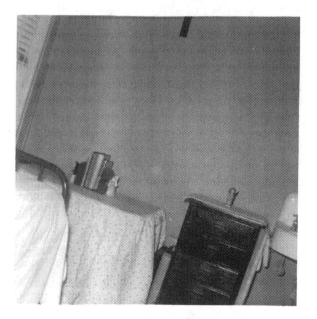

My convent bedroom

like all the other nuns, because it was against the rule for nuns to sit in comfortable chairs. We were only allowed to sit in hard wooden chairs. This is in line with the practice of mortification. Being uncomfortable was supposed to bring one closer to God.

Despite her age, Sister Anna's face was smooth and radiated a sense of peace and kindness. I could actually feel the holiness in her. She smiled and said, "Now, dear, find your cell, unpack your things, and get ready to come downstairs to the second-floor chapel for afternoon prayers. You have one and a half hours free before then." With her words, I could feel the tension slide off my shoulders. I was relieved that Sister seemed so very nice. She also pointed across the hall from her room to another bedroom. She had turned it into a storage room for all the nuns' supplies. Pretty cool, I thought. Sister Anna told me to help myself to anything I needed. This arrangement was wonderful and unheard of in the convent. Because of the vow of poverty, the rule stated that we were supposed to go on our knees and ask for anything that we might need. As I left, I peeked into the storage room. It had a single bed and several huge steel-locker cabinets. They were not locked.

I was a young nun. All the rest were older nuns, and I had heard that this was a very tough assignment due to the fact that the nuns were grouchy and did not care for young nuns. Right then and there, I decided to change things. I started being very nice and cunning and forced the nuns to hold conversations with me. One of the nuns had elephant man's disease (neurofibromatosis) in her face, and she looked like a monster. Whenever she went out, people would stare and run from her. I am jumping the story, but I succeeded after a few months to get that nun to like me and we became great friends. When my family came to visit once a month on a Sunday afternoon for two hours, my little niece, Therese, ran to Sister and hugged her. This made Sister very happy.

Sister Anna

The next day began my charge, taking care of Sister Anna. I prepared her for school and accompanied her over to her first-floor office in the school building. She walked very gingerly, holding onto the banister and my arm when we went down the stairs, and shuffled her feet on the ground as we made our way out the back door to her spacious principal's office. Once there, she positioned herself behind a large desk. Sister Anna was polite and very thankful for my help. Then I scurried off to teach first grade.

After teaching in the morning from nine to twelve, we returned to the convent for a hot lunch. Before eating, we had to go upstairs to the chapel for what was called the "Examination of Conscience." This took fifteen minutes. All the nuns had to mark a little blue book for any faults that they committed that morning. During this examination, Sister Anna stayed downstairs. After lunch we went back to the classroom for the afternoon session. I attended to her during these times also, helping her walk across to her office.

At the end of the school day, we were allowed to speak for an hour. Then the bell rang for us to stop talking and assemble in the community room for spiritual reading, followed by afternoon prayers and supper at six o'clock. Usually after that we had an hour to prepare our schoolwork for the next day. On Thursday and Sunday nights we were given an extra half hour to talk with other nuns and share plates of chocolate candy.

According to the ancient rules of the congregation, night prayers were always said about 8 PM in the chapel followed by "Sacred Silence." This special silence was offered to God nightly as another means of discipline. The Holy Rule said that no one was allowed to speak from 8 PM until after breakfast at 7:30 in the morning.

When night prayers ended, Sister Anna motioned for me to follow her. It was my job, or charge as it was called, to help her get ready for bed. She told me what she needed. I unhooked her veil and her habit dress. Then she went into the adjoining little bathroom next to her room and undressed and washed her body using a small shower. She put on her long nightgown and a white head cap. We all had to wear white caps on our heads when we went to bed at night.

Sister came back into the bedroom and sat in the big chair. She told me where to find a large metal bucket, which she instructed me to fill with soapy warm water so she could soak her feet. I placed both of her feet into the soapy water. Then, on my knees, I washed her legs and feet. As I did this, she began to speak. But later I was soon to learn that sitting in a comfy chair and speaking during the "Sacred Silence" were the least of Sister Anna's transgressions.

She asked me about my family and the other mission that I had come from. Sister asked if I would mind getting up before the other nuns every morning to help her get dressed. Technically, we were not supposed to be talking.

Each night, when everyone else had gone to bed, as I knelt at Sister Anna's feet, washing them, she would tell me stories of her childhood and early years in the convent. She had come from a wealthy family in Quebec. They owned a biscuit company in Canada and took annual vacation trips by horse-drawn carriage to Florida each year. On the way there, they always stopped for a break at a rest house that the nuns ran on Main Street, in Flushing, New York. It was here that young Anna met the nuns and joined that order when she was seventeen years old.

Sister Anna encountered the same lifestyle and training that I learned many years later. Apparently, time stood still in convent life. When we would ask why we had to do a certain thing, we always received the same answer: "We have done this from time immemorial."

It took only a few nights before Sister Anna revealed to me her own special methods for helping others.

After Sister Anna's two years of training, she was sent to work in a boys' orphanage in Rockaway, which was operated by her order of nuns. She noticed that the nun in charge of the kitchen was not giving adequate food to feed the six- and seven-year-old boys entrusted to Sister Anna's care.

This upset her greatly. Her life had been very good, and she despaired at seeing these boys—who had nothing to call their own—not even get enough to eat at the home for boys. She spoke to the nun about her concern. But instead of giving a little extra food to the boys as she had anticipated, the nun hollered at her. That's when Sister Anna decided to do things her way.

She secretly had her family arrange to sneak extra food into the convent. They had someone deliver it and leave it on her windowsill, where she made sure that the window was open. They also placed money into a bank account for her use. As was the custom in the evening, after the young boys got washed and into their pajamas, the bell would ring to signal the children to go with the nun in charge of them to her bedroom for night prayers. Going to the chapel was too long a walk and was cold for the children. Instead of praying with the little ones, she instructed them to be silent and distributed the food. They ate at her feet. When the bell for lights out rang, she turned the lights out but told the young boys to keep eating in the dark. She then took them back to their beds in the dorm. This became a nightly ritual. They were never caught. In fact, Sister packed lunches for the boys for school the next day because the nun in the kitchen gave every boy only one slice of bologna and a piece of bread.

The order of nuns had a home for young girls that the sisters also ran. Sister Anna regaled me with stories about her visits to this home in Flushing. There, Sister met a man named Mr. Bonofino, whose wife had passed away. Because he could not care for his two young daughters and work at the same time, he placed them in the home. Sister would meet the little girls when she went there on her many trips to attend meetings. She felt so sorry for these two young ones that she decided to take them under her wing. They became her special children. She put money away for them and watched over them. She helped the father with his rent. When it was time for the girls to go home, they had bank accounts in their names. Sister Anna told me she made sure the girls got the money in case the father remarried again. Smart woman, this Sister Anna. She told me that she made a will out and left a good amount to these lovely young ladies.

Now, as young women, the girls came to visit Sister Anna once a month. I would meet them and give them refreshments. Both were pretty and had long dark hair. Sister favored the younger of the two girls, whom she saw as more vulnerable. When they had to leave after their visit, Sister gave me extra money to put into the pocketbook of her favorite, making sure that the other one didn't see. It delighted me to be part of her spiritual life. The girls liked me because I took such good care of their beloved Sister.

Each night, as I knelt at the feet of Sister Anna, washing and rinsing, she instructed me how to help others breaking the rules where necessary. It reminded me of Jesus washing the feet of his apostles, except I was the follower, washing the feet of the holy one. It humbled me and stirred within me a deeper mission. I was to find ways to get around the rules to help others, but must try not to get caught.

I can do that, I thought.

13
Doing Sister Anna's Work

It quickly became apparent to me that Sister Anna was truly a unique and remarkable person—a woman far more liberated and empowered than any other who tried to work within this male-dominated environment of the church. Her kindness and patience belied her steely resolve in carrying out her mission, even if it meant working under the church's radar.

It was the first week in September. We had just come in from class, and I had helped Sister into her comfy chair and brought her tea and cookies. Her room was small, square like a box, consisting of her chair, a bed, and a clothes bureau. The light from the two large windows, one facing Putnam Avenue and the other facing Classon Avenue, let plenty of sunlight in, which made it a pleasant place for her to rest after school. It was around 3:30 PM. Afternoon prayers would begin at the sound of the large handheld bell at 4:45 PM.

Just as I was about to leave to rejoin the other nuns in the kitchen, Sister told me to sit on her bed, the only other place to sit in the room. She placed her teacup and saucer back on the tray and folded her hands in her lap. "My dear, please go on an errand for me," she said. "The sisters really enjoy those rolls in the morning. I need you to go to the bakery." She gave me directions to the nearest Ebinger's Bakery on Nostrand Avenue, about a mile away.

How could I go? I had not yet taken my first vows. The rules did not allow me, a novice without vows, out of the convent, except in particular circumstances and never alone. We had to go out in twos. Remember, "From time immemorial ..." But, I figured, she knew the rules, and besides, I was too timid to speak up.

When I got to the bakery, the lady behind the counter had the bag of rolls all ready for me. I did not have to wait in line, for she saw me coming in my habit. Who could miss that? She took no money and smiled as she handed me the bag.

The next morning at breakfast, I watched the nuns' faces as they devoured the rolls. I smiled. Anyone who's ever lived in Brooklyn remembers Ebinger's. I was brought up on Ebinger's rolls and cakes. I took this walk every day but Sunday, all year long, rain or snow.

It was during these walks to the bakery that I got to know the neighborhood in which I lived. The neighborhood was very poor and dangerous. The streets seemed to be languishing in despair. I passed burned-out buildings, women who kept their eyes down as we met, homeless men sleeping in the doorways, little babies roaming the sidewalks with an older child watching them, and families trying to exist in this godforsaken place. I wanted so much to help those I met. All I could do was smile for them.

As the weeks progressed, Sister Anna called me into her room again to give me another errand to run. This time she instructed me to go to a certain grocery store far away from our neighborhood, up near Prospect Park. The owner's name was Tony. I was to see only him—no one else. Sister had handwritten several lists of groceries for me to give to him. I looked at them, trying to decipher her shaky writing; her hand trembled due to her age.

I was a little shy going into his store the first time. I wondered why Sister had picked this cramped deli so far from our convent. But as soon as I entered, a small man with dark, closely cropped hair, piercing blue eyes, and a friendly smile approached me. This was Tony. He knew Sister Anna for years when she did errands for herself. Tony knew exactly why I stood before him.

Tony invited me to sit down in a chair and offered me a cream soda. I had walked a long way from the bakery and was tired. I appreciated his kindness. We never had soft drinks in the convent. The cream soda tasted wonderful.

There were at least thirty-five items on each list. He told me the total cost, and I paid him with the money in an envelope that Sister Anna had given me. I never knew who was receiving these bags of groceries. But all the recipients knew that the groceries would be delivered to their door that week.

Tony told me there were several poor families and some old men and women who lived nearby and appreciated this great help. So this was my ritual three times a week for the entire school year. I was late getting back for afternoon prayers and had to make them up after supper. I did not mind, for this was why I had entered the convent— to help others. I was Sister's Anna's feet to do her bidding.

Not one of the sisters ever questioned Sister Anna about my walks. They knew about the rolls, and that was my excuse. Along the way, as I said before, I made friends with many people, for I would see the same people daily. One day I met a pretty young lady of about twenty. She was new to the neighborhood and was pushing a stroller with twin girls in it. This young woman came over and introduced herself to me as Gloria. She had just come up from the south and was trying desperately to find a job. She was a single mother. I met her daily, but she was not having much luck in her life. Then for a long time, I did not see her. One day, to my sorrow, I saw her pushing the girls, who were now a little older. She was on drugs, and her face was covered with pimples. Gloria did not recognize me. I felt extremely sad. I was beginning to understand that I could not help everyone I met. I had to understand that our lives are like a circle and we can only help some within that circle. Sister Anna certainly understood this.

We had a large influx of people from Puerto Rico who settled in our neighborhood. Since they had just arrived, most of them were very poor, and most were Catholic. One day I was standing outside our Catholic school. The parents of some of these children from Puerto Rico approached me. The wind was blowing, and winter was approaching. Two mothers had old ripped coats that they hugged about their body. I smiled at them. They nervously moved toward me, then away. It seemed they needed encouragement to approach me. I motioned for them to come over. In fractured English, they said they could not afford the clothes for the First Communion ceremony for their little ones.

It struck me as odd that here in the middle of this poverty-stricken neighborhood we had a school that catered to the middle- and upper-class from another neighborhood. The poor in our own neighborhood could not afford to pay the tuition. They came to religious classes after school instead. I stressed that they should not worry about the clothes—I would lay out a plan to dress their children. The young mothers seemed very happy as I watched them skipping down the block, singing. I knew Sister Anna would be happy with my decision.

In those days, every child had to be dressed in white for the occasion. How could we assist these children? I had a plan and talked it over with Sister Anna during our nightly ritual. She gave me money for the dresses for the little girls, and shirts and trousers for the boys, which I purchased from a clothing factory in Manhattan.

The children now had their outfits for First Holy Communion, but they also needed white shoes for the occasion. Our pastor was a cranky man, so it was out of the question to ask for his help. Instead, I approached a young priest who was assigned to work in our parish rectory. I told him my plan. On Tuesday afternoon, he was to keep a watch on the pastor while I went in the side door of the rectory. I knew the closet where the money from the Sunday collections was kept. My plan was to take enough money out of the baskets to buy shoes for the children for their First Holy Communion. The priest simply shrugged, as if to say, "Sure, why not?"

Tuesday arrived. This was the day that I instructed the little ones for Communion. I ran into the rectory about three o'clock, as was planned, and took a bunch of bills. I did not even stop to count them—just stuffed them in my large nun pockets and ran out. I told the children in my class to stand up and follow me and be very quiet.

It was certainly a scene to see me leading about twenty little ones down the block. I walked fast, and they tried to keep up. The children had no idea where we were going. I felt like the Piped Piper leading the children out of town.

The week before, I had taken a quick walk down to the avenue to case the children's shoe store. That was where we were now headed— and running fast so we would not be caught. Perhaps I would end up in jail, but these children would have their shoes for their First Holy Communion.

We crossed the street holding hands, and I motioned for the children to enter the store and take seats. With a wave of my hand, I directed the workers to hurry and fit the children with white shoes. I asked that they also give each child white socks. It was a rare sight as the workers ran back and forth measuring then fitting the little girls and boys. The children's faces were beaming.

When the bill came, I dug deep into my pocket, and all the bills came falling to the ground. The store owner just stared at me slack-jawed as I scrambled to pick up the bills. I counted out the bills one by one until I had enough to pay for the shoes. I had a little left over, but what was I going to do with it? I certainly couldn't risk getting caught putting it back. I would let Sister Anna help me on that one.

Mission accomplished. Off we went, hurriedly again, back up to the school building, each little one carrying a bag with precious cargo inside.

That night I told Sister Anna what had transpired. She relished hearing me describe the children's faces as they tried on their new shoes. She also had a great suggestion for what to do with the extra money: I would throw the children a party.

A few months later, I got another assignment. I was enjoying milk and cookies with the other sisters after school one day, when Sister Anna summoned me. I took the stairs two at a time, for I had a lot of energy. When I got to her door, she motioned me to come in and sit on the edge of her bed. She was sitting in her large lounge chair. The sister whose job it was to do the shopping and planning of meals for the convent was sick and had to return to the motherhouse. Sister Anna asked me, "Sister, do you think you would mind taking over this job, and I will assist you?" I replied, "I will be glad to do this, if you will show me how."

Now it was my charge to buy the food and plan the meals for the convent. Sister Anna insisted that I serve the nuns the very best food. She was a very small eater, but we had several older nuns on special diets. I catered to them, and they were happy. Sister Anna was very good in making out food lists, so all I had to do was deliver the lists to the local grocery store on Fulton Street. The manager met me the first time I went and explained that the food he had in his store was not good. He would take the list home to where he lived, fill it from his neighborhood store, and deliver it to the convent the next day.

What I learned was that the poor had no choice but to buy food of below-standard quality, and at higher prices. I was sad about this but could do or say nothing at the time.

One day, Sister noticed a person at our side kitchen door begging for food. She immediately told me to feed him a big meal. I guess word got around the neighborhood. The next evening, the kitchen doorbell rang, and there were five poorly dressed men standing there on the stoop when I answered. I went into the dining room, for it was suppertime. I told Sister Anna. She came out and looked. Then she turned and instructed me to feed them. Furthermore, I was to purchase food to feed twenty extra people every night, just in case more men showed up at our door.

These men told me they were veterans. They slept in the streets or in the subway stations. From that day on, my job was to plan to have Sister Rose, our cook, prepare extra food so that we could provide hot meals for these poor men. I often think that my doing this was the first "fast-food joint" in the city.

At six every evening, I left my place in the chapel and went downstairs to the kitchen to prepare the plates. We purchased paper plates and plastic utensils for their use. It was worth all the trouble I went through to hear, "Thank you, Sis." They often told me that "Sis" treated them better than the Salvation Army. Sister Anna made believe that she had no part in this. She left it in my hands, and that was the end of it. I know she was pleased, though, when I'd recount the men's expressions of gratitude for the food while washing her feet at night.

On my many trips to the local stores, my homeless friends protected me as I moved through the drug-infested areas of Bedford-Stuyvesant. I was their "Sis." I never thought to worry about my walks, for these men were on every corner and always watched out for me. One day, a stray dog started to attack me, probably because of my long skirt fluttering about. There on the corner was one of my friends. I ran into his arms so he could protect me from this stray mutt barking ferociously at me. It worked. He shouted the dog away, and I thanked him and went on my way.

Not only was Sister Anna a just and caring person, she liked to be in control even while ignoring the rules. The rules stated that there was to be no visiting other convents. We were not to have any special friends. Sister Anna, believe it or not, managed for years to celebrate her feast day once a year at the end of June, when all the nuns were off from school.

I helped her prepare for weeks for this function. She had invited sixty of her nun friends. In amazement, I watched her work as she thought only of giving joy to others. I knew they all would bring her nice gifts, even though this was against the rules.

She ordered the caterers to set up about twelve round tables in our dining room. Each table had a white linen tablecloth and napkins on it. Sister had ordered roses for the center of each table.

The doorbell rang. I answered it, and the florist delivered twelve dozen long-stemmed red roses—a dozen for the center of each table. They were beautiful. It was a very hot day, and the florist instructed me to keep them in a cool place. It would be two hours before the party began. I did not want the roses to wilt, so I placed the twelve dozen rose arrangements into our gigantic freezer! What did I know? I had never received roses in my life.

When it came time to take the roses out and place them on the tables, they were all dead—frozen! I was so scared. I had to tell Sister Anna. I went up the stairs to her bedroom, shaking. As usual, she was sitting in her comfy chair. I told her what I had done. Imagine my surprise when she said to me, "Well, dear, you will just have to order twelve dozen more." Not another word was spoken. I bounced down the stairs and did exactly that, and the flowers arrived before the guests.

All the invited nuns carried gifts. We served the guests wine and a big special meal in our dining room. (By the way, wine was forbidden). Sister Anna decided not to come downstairs. She told me she just wanted to hear the happy laughter of the nuns having a great time. What a lovely party for Sister Anna as she sat upstairs in her comfortable chair. I often thought that she paid off the Reverend Mother so the party could take place.

The gifts were displayed in the community room. They included lovely pieces of artwork, linen tablecloths, blankets, and silverware. I was amazed at the expensive items. In the evening, I packed up the gifts and brought them into Sister Anna's room. The next morning, she motioned me to come into her room. Whatever was she going to do with these gifts? It was not in keeping with our vow of poverty.

"Dear," she said, "you are such a help to me. Please take all of those gifts and give them to your family on visiting day." My mouth dropped open. The next visiting day, I had placed all the gifts in the parlor for my family to take home. My sisters loved Sister Anna.

My life was becoming intertwined with that of Sister Anna's. There were canonical rules that we were obliged to follow, rules that hadn't changed since the fifteenth century when our order was founded in France. Silence, mortification, spiritual readings, and studying the Bible were woven into our lives, like the stiff starched poplin linens and heavy black serge robes of our habit.

We pledged to seek a perfect ideal not only by our three sacred vows (poverty, chastity, and obedience), but also by our personal humility and charity. It seemed that we were linked to those who served before us by the same set of rules. Shaven heads, hair shirts, physical punishment of our own bodies, starvation, mortification— you name it, we did it. At the end of the week, the holy rule had another practice for us to obey. We had to assemble on Saturday evening and go before the superior on our knees and confess out loud our transgressions of the week. Everyone would be listening.

Sister Anna taught me to realize that nothing is perfect—not the church, nuns, or humanity. She taught me to get around these practices and rules and still keep my great compassion and deep conviction to help others.

At night as I knelt before her, we talked about the day that had just passed. She would instruct me on how to handle things, and she planned the next day with me. Each night I heard new stories, and they inspired me. We were also breaking the rule of Sacred Silence together—a young nun and her old superior.

14
Letting the Outside World In

I had not taken my vows. The vows of poverty, chastity, and obedience were taken after three years of training. Then they would be renewed each year for three years until we made our final vows. The rule did not allow me out of the convent, and never alone. We had to go out in twos. Remember, "From time immemorial ..."

Coming home from one of my daily walks to Ebinger's, I heard a shout from two blocks away—"Hey, Cuz." I kept walking, with my habit moving about my legs. It sounded again. I turned, hesitantly, and looked back. It was my cousin, Billy Flaherty. He was a policeman patrolling the streets of that neighborhood. Our families were close growing up. Our fathers had come from Ireland together on the same boat and went through Ellis Island together. Billy and I hung around in the same crowd. We were the two wild ones, always getting in trouble with the families. His mother, Margaret, and my mom were best friends.

Once, at our graduation party from elementary school, four of our families that were related had one big party. There were the O'Briens, the Flahertys, the O'Tooles, and the Flemings. They assigned the kids to the second floor of the brownstone in Park Slope, and the adults were downstairs. Billy asked me to go downstairs and ask my uncle, Paddy O'Brien, to give me a little jigger of whiskey for Billy. I did. Paddy smiled and gave it to me. Billy enjoyed it. There was a big family argument about this, and it caused two of the families not to talk for years. Billy and I laughed, but then we also felt guilty.

Now, here was Billy, running up the block to me. He wanted to know what I was doing walking in such a bad neighborhood by myself. I told him. He walked me back to the convent. We had so much fun. He promised that we would do it again when he was assigned there. Actually Billy alerted all the cops to be on the lookout for me. I felt like skipping but could not, since nuns had to demonstrate "proper decorum."

I arrived back at the convent and went up to tell Sister Anna that I was home and had met my cousin Billy. She smiled. It must have been difficult for her. She was once a very vibrant, active person and now she could not get around too well, so she sat in her room with the door open. We would wave or smile as we passed by. Sister would sit there looking at the world outside, from her two large windows, praying or reading.

Sister Anna was a gentle soul who went out of her way to make us feel very happy in her convent.

Shortly after school opened that September, a kind couple donated a large-screen television set to the convent. We were so excited and happy. It would be so very good for the older nuns, to say nothing about me. Sister Anna had it hooked up, and we were allowed to watch it during the evening hours. What a treat! It didn't last long. Some miserable person snitched on us to the General Superior, who was the head of the entire order. A letter arrived stating, "There will be no televisions in the convents. It is against the rule. This has been from time immemorial."

Sister Anna showed me the letter but told me to keep it a secret for a while. About a month later, Sister sadly posted the letter on the bulletin board. Two days after that, Sister came into the community room. We had just finished watching our favorite show. She had a big blanket and just threw it over the set. There it stayed for years.

We lived in a poverty-stricken area. Our convent was assigned an old Irish nun to do our cooking for us. Usually the convent hired someone to prepare the midday hot meal, but in this area they sent Sister Rose to us. She was a very lovely, humble old person who wished to be a cook in the convent. She came from Ireland and entered our order of nuns. She was offered the opportunity to become a teacher but her wish was to cook for the nuns in the convent. Sister Rose was a very loving, humble older person who added to the joy in our house. Her cooking was good and Sister Anna gave her anything that she requested to prepare the meals for us.

15
Breaking the Color Barrier

I was beginning to realize that Sister Anna was guiding my life. She taught me that I would see much human weakness. I must empathize with these weaknesses and continue the work for the Lord. Sister Anna was a powerful person in her own right, having lived her life of great compassion and deep convictions. Sister was like an immovable stone in her old age, seeing that there was still so much that she could do. She was determined to do it through me.

Most of the convents were run by very strict superiors. The group of novices that I entered with was called a "party." When we came out on a mission, we met once a month at the school for teachers run by the diocese. My friends would tell me stories that were unbelievable. Some superiors would not allow the novices to talk to anyone. Soap was considered a luxury. Food was meager, and supplies were nil. If the young nuns broke any rules, they were subjected to fierce penances. Some penances doled out were to kneel in the chapel for an hour or to kneel in front of the superior for an hour in front of the rest of the community. Some superiors would cancel visiting by parents, which was scheduled by the rule once a month. It went on and on.

I considered myself lucky, for I was out there doing my good work while my friends were being subjected to really inhumane treatment. These superiors at the time were superiors for life, so they did not worry that anything could happen to them. They could break any rules and make living under their leadership very difficult. We had names for some of them—Sister Gorilla, Sister Monster, and others that I cannot say now. We lived in fear of being sent to those places of horror.

My family on monthly visiting day

Of course, I could not tell of my walking the walk. Usually most nuns taught classes and had their prayer life. I was so busy after teaching with my running around to help others that I was starting to realize how wonderful this old nun was as she started to end her days as I sat at her feet and learned her ways.

One time my good mother came to see me alone, arriving in a taxicab, for my father was working. It was my birthday, and Sister Anna gave her permission to visit for two hours. This was definitely against the rules. Birthdays were not to be celebrated in the convent. My mother came to the convent carrying boxes of cakes from Ebinger's. She knew we all loved Ebinger's cakes. After her visit, we were walking up the main street to flag down a cab for her trip home. As we walked, she said to me, "Eileen, I hope you never come out on these streets—they are so dangerous!" "No, Mom," I answered.

"Don't you worry about me!" Just then we approached seven shabbily dressed men hanging out on the corner and sitting in the doorways. They all stood up and said, "Hi, Sis!" My mother was visibly upset to think this was what she raised me for.

As time went on, I began to feel more secure in my freedom. I realized I now could do things for people and then tell Sister Anna. It was a mature feeling and very good for me as a young nun.

Willie was five years old, and both of his parents worked all day. They lived across the street from the convent. Willie had very bad asthma. His attacks were always very serious, so when he had one and couldn't breathe, he came to his window on the third floor and knocked wildly. The grownups and kids on the street would come running to the convent screaming, "Sis, Willie, Willie, Willie!"

I had permission to run over to his apartment and quickly give him his medicine. I loved Willie. He was the first young black male—at age six—to be allowed in our all-white school. This was done with Sister Anna's guidance. "Just keep it quiet, put him in your class so that you can take care of him during the day, and get the medicine from his parents to administer to him."

I talked so much about Willie that my mother and Aunt Katie attended all the school functions in which Willie participated. Willie was a fine, handsome young man. You couldn't help but love him. At the time, I did not realize it, but we started the first integration process in Nativity School and no one was the wiser.

We also had to go out in public in twos. That was the rule. Why? Well, I was told the answer is in the Bible. "When Christ sent his apostles out, he sent them "two by two"—therefore, we, 2000 years later, had to do the same thing. Sister Anna said nothing about this rule. She just sent me wherever she wanted me to be.

We had to walk unless the distance was too far. When I was taking classes downtown, we took the bus and got bus fare to ride. As we were boarding the bus, we were praying that the bus driver would not take our money. Then we could call our parents from a public phone at the university. A big smile came over my face as the bus driver placed his hand over the fare box, meaning, "You do not have to pay on this bus, Sister." That is why, years later, after I left the convent, I always had a big smile on my face for the bus drivers; they probably figured that I was flirting with them.

One Saturday I had to walk to classes about twenty blocks away, down to Saint Joseph's College. I do not remember why I was alone, but I do remember coming home near dusk and seeing a big, horrible man with a meat cleaver in his hand, chopping on a man's body that was sprawled on the sidewalk. If I ran, he would certainly overtake me. It was like a movie; everyone was slowly slinking away to safety. Keeping calm would give me more time to plan, I figured. Then a car came, and he went after the driver. I got away, held up my skirts, and went flying home to the convent. Sister Anna was standing at her window watching, feeling helpless. She hugged me when I came in. I am sure that the driver was okay and got away safely. He must have stopped to distract that man just to save me. I prayed for that person. Sister Anna told me to make a cup of tea for myself and go to my room to rest. She exempted me from my prayers that night.

Stefan and Alonzo Sherman were the next two boys enrolled. Their mother was a young friend of mine. I had met her during my daily walks through the neighborhood. She had taken them down south for a visit but came right back when she realized the south at that time was terribly biased. Her boys could not use the bathrooms for whites or drink from whites' water fountains or be served in white areas of restaurants. She wanted the best for her two young sons. Our neighborhood was not entirely poor, and there were some lovely homes and nice families living there. Usually the people did not feel welcome in our parish or school.

During our nightly talks, I mentioned how nice Stefan and Alonzo were. I wished they could be in our school. Sister told me to tell the mother to come up quietly to her office some day. Mrs. Sherman came up within two days. Sister registered the boys into our school without telling the pastor. Stefan was put into my class, and Alonzo was placed in the second grade. I was so happy, as were the mother and the boys. Now they wanted to become altar boys. I told them to sign up for the altar boy class.

Usually it took one or two months at the most to learn how to serve at Mass. One must recall that the pastor had helped build a special school for blacks around the corner. How was he going to allow these young boys to go on the altar? They were in the altar boy class for one year and, of course, as expected, were not allowed to serve. I was furious. I was feeling very powerful in my ways due to having Sister Anna on my side. Their lovely mother was going to take them out of the altar boy class. I insisted they stay.

I had a plan. They were to be the first, and I would help them fight the system. A young priest had just been assigned to our parish. I told Sister Anna. She gave me permission to meet with him and talk to him about this problem. I met with him and explained what was happening. That week, they were told to serve Mass. Of course, it was done, and the pastor could not say a thing. Sister Anna and I sat at the six-thirty Mass smiling away.

As the years went by, Sister told me that I could sneak home for the day. This happened several times a year. The rule said that I could not go home for six years, and then only once a year. I could not tell anyone, for she would be in trouble. I took the bus home and had a wonderful time. My parents were so happy. My brother-in-law, Tom, would drive me back to the convent at five PM, but he had to let me off two blocks from the convent so no one would know or see us. Sister Anna watched this from her window and was so happy for me. That was really cool—she was some lady, so soft and kind.

Convent building in Brooklyn

My two favorite altar boys

We were never allowed alcoholic beverages. The only time that I wanted something strong was when I had bad cramps from my period. She would tell me to just go into the storeroom next door and help myself. I usually took enough to knock me out for the night. She treated all the nuns in this fashion. She trusted us and respected us.

By comparison the next superior was not that way. We would have to ask for Kotex or Tampax and Sister Adele would hand you *one*. We were horrified. It was humiliating to ask. However, I planned that my mom would come when the superior was out of the house, which she was every Saturday. My great mom delivered two big cartons, and I hid them and told everyone where they were. Sister Adele never inquired as to why we didn't ask her for napkins anymore. Knowing her, she probably thought that we all had an early "change of life."

This type of life with Sister Anna lasted six years. My work continued as I walked the streets of Bedford-Stuyvesant, helping the poor, feeding the hungry, and visiting the sickly and lonely and elderly. I was extremely happy doing this work. One time Sister sent me over to an old lady's home. The lady just sat there. Her husband had died years before, and nothing was changed. She showed me all around the house, how the clock stayed at that hour of death, the book opened, and the calendar the same. I found it a bit spooky. I did not like to go there.

There are so many stories that I find it difficult to put them all in this book.

Nothing lasts forever. Being young, one thinks not of the future but of the present. This is an important part of young life. I never imagined life without Sister Anna. I guess I never even entertained the thought. However, one day, Sister was not feeling well. We called an ambulance, and they took her out on a stretcher. I remember standing, staring at that old body, dressed in her habit, as the person with the ambulance insisted that we keep her head down. I asked them, "Why?" They explained that this would stop the internal bleeding. I was so upset. I guess I knew we would not have her back with us. I figured this was the end.

The nun in charge just announced that Sister was to retire to the "old nun's" home in Flushing. It was indeed a very sad day for all of the nuns in the convent—doubled by the fact that the superior who came shortly to take Sister Anna's place was a mean, severe woman. However, Sister Muriel de Lourdes, who was Sister Anna's dear friend, came to see us shortly after. She took me aside and told me that Sister Anna was going to be all right but needed an easier life. I felt better about that but cried in Sister Muriel's arms.

16
New Superior

The new superior was not a nice person. I wanted nothing to do with her. The nuns insisted that I continue as the superior's helper. They claimed this would make our living easier, knowing her reputation. If I could pull some strings, our life would be better. I really was not in the mood. Then I saw some things that really made me angry. Remember, I was young and trained by Sister Anna for justice.

The new person stopped me from doing the buying. This meant she was going to buy all the food and plan the meals. She gave us little to eat. As for herself, Sister was always going out to dinner with her sister, who was a single woman. I remember one time I went down to the grocery store to complain to the manager that he was giving Sister Adele decaying vegetables for the convent. He answered me, "Sister, I do not give it to her; she asks for what I am discarding. Then she puts it in a shopping bag and takes it home to the convent." I felt this nun was either not too swift or just mean. On Saturday nights, she would come in after spending the day with her sister and would share with me what she had eaten in her favorite restaurant, Gage and Tollner's, located on Fulton Street in Brooklyn. I knew it to be a really expensive, nice place to eat.

Well, it was here where I stepped in. Having been trained by Sister Anna, I knew the ropes. I could steal food and sneak in anything that the nuns might need. Looking in on this scene will bring smiles to anyone who reads this part. The older nuns really appreciated me at this point, and we all drew closer together as a result of Sister Adele. I was in charge of selling candy to the school. Since very little food was available to us, I had to go to work again to be nice to Sister Adele. In the meantime, I would steal the candy money, buy sandwiches, and distribute them to the other nuns at three o'clock when she left the school building to go back to the convent to count her money. I was very good at doing these things. I would let the superior think that she could trust me, and I got away with a lot. Some of the other nuns were too scared or too holy to do what I would do. Sister Anna had taught me well.

The convent had a dumbwaiter going from the basement to the third floor where our bedrooms were. I used it to send food that I bought with the candy money upstairs. One day, the darn cord broke. On the dumbwaiter were hero sandwiches and ice cream sodas. What to do? I put black soot on my face and went into her room on the second floor. All the other nuns went to hide in their rooms. I made believe that I was crying because I had broken the dumbwaiter. I asked for a penance. She said, "Dear, never go near that thing again. Lock it with nails. It is dangerous." So to this day, I guess, there are the remains of our supper hiding in those walls.

It was a very difficult year, trying to appease her, and be nice when I felt like telling her off. But I survived, and we had many laughs about our situation. It was a common situation in many convents, but they did not have someone on the staff trained by Sister Anna.

17
Blessed Are the Poor

Sister Muriel de Lourdes was Sister Anna's best friend and sidekick. She was the woman who took Sister to the bank every Saturday to get money for good works. The orders came on August 15. Sister Muriel was made superior down the road at 895 Putnam Avenue. The name of the parish was Our Lady of Good Counsel. She immediately requested Reverend Mother to send me to her convent. I had no idea this was to happen. We had no say in these decisions. I was happy to get out of where I was. Now I was moving deeper into Bedford-Stuyvesant. Sister Muriel was great and a lot of fun—and she was to have Sister Anna live in our convent every weekend. My sad time was over, and I was about to blossom into my full personality.

Sister Muriel encouraged me to continue to work with the poor. This convent had several young nuns, and that was a wonderful change for me. We embarked on many works to help others. What a wonderful superior! She was younger than Sister Anna. Sister Muriel had a great humorous way with us, and we laughed a lot. The religious brothers who taught the boys were also a delight to work with, and the pastor was superb. These were my happiest days as a nun—at last. The pastor used to say that whenever he passed the convent, he would hear us laughing. It was so true.

I ran one of the first summer Head Start programs in Brooklyn. It was a huge success, but not because of me; we all worked together, and that was the secret. The teachers were the young students from St. Joseph's Teachers' College, and I was called the "director." It was a nice feeling to be able to use my talents freely. Whenever we had a young child that was crying, I would call for Brother Mario, the principal of the boys' department, to come over from the friary. He would take the child in his arms and walk the halls with him until the crying stopped.

Sister Anna spent every weekend during the entire summer with us. I would tell her of all that I was doing, and she would be so happy for me. Her advice was well taken. All she wanted was her banana and sugar and milk for breakfast. I had to walk blocks during the day to get a decent banana. I would not let her down.

My classroom, where I taught my first grade boys, was up on the fourth floor. It was my assignment each morning before classes started to put a big American flag out on the pole by use of a pulley. What a scary feeling, to lean out and pull on this rope. On the morning of the "Bay of Pigs," I put the flag out, not knowing that I put it out upside down—a sign of distress. Also, we were not aware of what was going on in Cuba. Within five minutes, about fifty policemen, firemen, and EMS workers were running up the four flights of stairs and into my classroom. I had no idea what was going on until they told me. I was embarrassed. The authorities did not think it was funny, because of what was happening that day. Sister Muriel just looked at me and said nothing.

The Franciscan Brothers were always sending us treats. Sister Muriel loved them, and we all enjoyed their gifts. Whenever Sister Muriel had to send something over to the boys' school, she used two of my little boys to go to the boys' school's principal's office. They had to go across the courtyard. We would watch them as they crossed over to the other school. The yard was enclosed, but we were very careful of the students under our charge. The little boys always came back eating ice cream, carrying a brown paper bag for us. Inside was an ice cream pop for Sister Muriel and another for me.

One of the nuns got jealous. The brother saw her standing in the school yard. He knew that she would take the bag from the children. Oh, God, you know what he did? He put a dead fish in the bag and watched as she stuck her hand in the bag to get ice cream. You know what she got! When he told us the story, I thought Sister Muriel and I would die laughing. The other nun never knew how to smile, so I figured it suited her well.

Sister Anna knew that I had more freedom here, and she was happy to see me involved. I was in charge of the school lunch program, which fed eight hundred students. I ordered a thousand free lunches daily. After school I packed up all the remaining food in bags. I remember it was very hard work. It had to be done quickly so that the food would not go bad. Sister Muriel gave me permission to hand-deliver it to the poor families that lived nearby. Old people received it, and anyone I knew that was really deserving of it. We had many Cuban refugees who had just arrived from Cuba. They really appreciated it as they received milk, juices, meats, and fruits for their families. Again, "Thank you, Sis" was the response. I wanted to tell them that Sister Anna trained me well.

Jorge Lopez came into my life and into my heart. He and his parents had just succeeded in getting out of Cuba. They had been wealthy but had only ten dollars when they arrived on our shores. Castro took all their goods. They were afraid Castro would send their only son to Russia to be trained in warfare, so they got out. Jorge arrived in my class. He was a gifted child. Castro certainly would have used him to his advantage at that time. The mother had been educated in Washington, DC as a teacher, so we hired her to teach in our school. The father was an engineer and was looking for work. We had to find a place in a school for the gifted for their son. When they got on their feet, they moved to Chicago. We kept in touch for a while. I later heard that Jorge became a musician.

I was very happy with my new mission. Here for five wonderful years, I was free to become totally immersed in community works from teenage clubs to beauty classes for young girls to young mothers' child-rearing classes. Anything that we wanted to initiate, anything that needed to be done, we were given permission to do.

This building, deep into Bedford-Stuyvesant, was a row building. We were living like the people we served. Our home looked the same, and we started to become friendly with all our neighbors. People did not realize that there were many marvelous folks living in Bedford-Stuyvesant.

Our convent was the last building attached to the other brownstones on Putnam Avenue. After that there was a walkway and then the large church building. By the other side of the church was the rectory where the priests lived. These priests were a caring and prayerful group of men who were dedicated to the people in our parish. On the other side of the rectory was the friary building, with about twelve brothers who ran the boys' school. We had a lot of fun with the brothers. Since their life was not as strict as ours, they made sure to send us treats and meals. On their feast day, wine and a large jug of manhattans would be delivered to our convent.

Sister Anna arrived on Friday in the car from the convent in Flushing, and she was picked up Monday morning to be taken back to the rest home in Flushing. At this point, I was doing my own work and telling her about it. She would just smile and be so happy for me. I know that she helped Sister Muriel financially. We did not have much money in this convent. The parish was a poor one. Once I got permission to sew lovely nylon curtains for the twelve large windows in the community room. I know who paid for them. Another time, I told Sister Muriel that our cells were disgraceful and needed painting.

I started to paint my own walls in my bedroom on the sneak. I had asked my father to bring me some paint, a paintbrush, and rolls of brillo to stuff in the space between the walls and the floor so mice could not get in. We had mice in the kitchen until I asked for an exterminator. Sister Muriel smelled the paint and then decided to have the entire place painted. I know that Sister Anna was really fussy about things, and Sister Muriel was easygoing. I guess Sister Anna told her to get it painted and she would pay. I was so used to getting things from Sister Anna, but now I had to go through Sister Muriel. It was strange, but she was so easy and really did everything that we asked.

All we had to do was tell her where we were after school. She gave us open permission to do whatever works we wanted to do. I started the first all-girls' track team in the Police Athletic League. I went to the track meets with the girls. I remember many times the weather was cold or rainy. Policemen would come over and cover me with their heavy coats. All I had to wear was a heavy shawl. When I look back at all of this, I feel very fortunate to have encountered all of these nice individuals.

During my spare time, I also worked as a drug counselor in the local police station. I remember the police detective in charge of the teenagers who were brought in. What a job he did daily. He was so happy to have me at a desk to help him with the girls they brought into the station house. This man impressed me. He had been doing this tough work for twenty years. After a year, he informed me he was retiring to California. I missed him a lot. His name was Sal.

When it was time to get Sister Anna to bed in her guest room, I entertained her with the stories of the work I was doing. She was very old now and smiled. I told her about the food from the lunch program that I delivered every afternoon to the poor families. Single mothers, old people, many people newly arrived from Cuba—and I would give some packages to the homeless along Fulton Street. In this convent, the poor did not come to the front door. Once in a while, though, someone from the neighborhood would ring the front doorbell asking for food. We always gave it to them.

Sister Muriel was different than Sister Anna because she was a little younger. However, she had the same mindset, and that was to help all those we could. She was very good to the nuns under her care. I did so much for Sister Muriel that she appreciated it by allowing me greater freedom. Once a week, she would ask me to go to New York City with her. We were supposed to be shopping for things for the convent. One time, we walked down the block, and Sister waved down a cab. She told him to take us to a point in the city that she knew. When we arrived, she took me into a restaurant, and we had dinner. I know that Sister Anna told her to do this as a treat for the two of us. I really enjoyed it.

Sister Muriel did not always go along with our thoughts. I was not afraid to convince her otherwise at times. We had a lovely black teenager in our school that kept running away from home. I asked her to come to me the next time. She did. Her father had cut her face with a knife, and I took her in at midnight. Sister Muriel was angry at me for answering the door and getting us all involved. I told her that was what we were there for. It was not to have a nice life but to help others. She relented but still was not thrilled.

The father came banging at the convent door looking for his daughter. I held her in my arms behind a couch in the parlor. Both of us were shaking with fear, but we made it through the crisis, as Sister Muriel came down and told him to disappear. We contacted her relatives in another state, and she moved there.

Manuel was in my first grade class but had to stay home all the time to care for his sick mother. I had gotten friendly with his mother when she stood outside the school-yard gates every morning watching as her two sons were in line to go into class. She was a very good mother and watched out for her sons. Whenever I asked, Manuel told me he could not come to class. His father worked two jobs to pay $500 a month rent to an absentee landlord for a house that had two floors. I decided to investigate.

Sister Muriel watched my class as I took Jose (Manuel's brother) down to investigate. The entrance to the house was through a basement window, and the only room that was livable was in the corner of the second floor. The family lived, cooked, and slept in that single room. I was shocked to see such a mess. I held up my skirts for fear that a rat would run up my legs under my skirt. I was only twenty-six years old at the time, and as I held that lovely mother in my arms, she closed her eyes and died. I cried for a long time, as did the boys. Later we went out the same way, leaving a note for the father to come to the convent. I took her two young sons out of that mess. Oh, God, why was there so much suffering and so little that I could do about it?

Across the street from our convent lived a lovely eighty-two-year-old black lady who was my friend. She had graduated from Hunter College with her PhD years before. Her sons came to visit her with their children, but now she lived alone in a big three-story brownstone. This grandmother's name was Mrs. Clarke. I knocked on her door and asked if she would take the two little boys in for a few days; it lasted six months until I managed to get placement for them in an upstate home for boys run by the Dominican nuns. The home for boys was crowded, but I had a friend up there and she took them in for me. Their father soon got a room nearby. The funeral director wanted $2,000 for the funeral expenses for the boys' mother.

I fought furiously against that and succeeded in the director doing it for a small fee, with our pastor paying for it.

I corresponded with the boys weekly and sent them care packages with Sister Muriel's approval. Later, when we got a new superior, she stopped all this letter writing. I had to ask the brothers to take over for a while, and they graciously did that job. I often wonder how Manuel and Jose's life turned out.

We had such nice students in our school. After school, each of the nuns had a club. Every afternoon after school, I planned that our children would have a choice of clubs. The eighth grade girls formed a beauty club, where we met once a week to learn how to fix hair and do makeup and nails. I remember I invited two women from Clairol to come and speak to us. They arrived, and it was a great afternoon. Only I did not realize that they got paid for this, and I had no money. Immediately I picked up my skirts and ran over to Sister Muriel with my problem. She just took money—which was from Sister Anna—and gave me fifty dollars for each of the women. I ran back and passed the brothers in the hallway of the school. They just smiled, for they really were amazed at all we were doing.

Another afternoon, I formed a club for the young students in grades one through three. The boys and girls that joined had to be on the honor roll. I figured this would encourage many of our students to work hard. They did, and their parents cooperated fully with us for it was after school. The children had milk and cookies. After that, we started our modern interpretive dancing session. I had learned this type of dancing in my high school. The children were to be picked up at school by 5 PM. I loved this class, and the children were so good that we put on shows for the parish and even appeared at local high schools and

Sisters Lydia, myself, and Muriel

colleges. We were invited to perform at the World's Fair. I still have
pictures taken at those shows.

We needed costumes. I went into the garment center and begged
for show dresses for the little girls and outfits for the boys. I did not
get them free but at a very good price that the parents could afford.

One time I remember, I was escorting my dance class to see a
play at Saint Joseph's College. We were on a bus when an Orthodox
Jewish rabbi, with a big black hat and a long black coat, got on. He
had curls down the side of his face. He sat down, and the children
were starting to giggle at the sight of him. I managed to give them a
stern look. I felt sorry for the rabbi. Then I thought, *My God, Eileen,
you also look funny with your long black robe and veil.* I wondered what
he was thinking.

The years passed quickly. I had been sent to college and earned
a BBA in business. Even though I told the order when asked that
I liked the work that I was doing, they decided to educate me to
teach business in high school. I continued teaching first grade in the
parish school called Our Lady of Good Counsel in Brooklyn. After
school hours were over, the other nuns and I were involved in various
activities working with the people of our neighborhood. It was my

home, there in Bedford-Stuyvesant, and I was happy. Sister Muriel and Sister Anna were a great help to all of us.

Sister Muriel's office was right next to my classroom. She was a great assistance if I needed to leave class or go on a trip. By the same token, I helped her run the school. Sister Muriel was now getting older and appreciated the expertise that I had achieved with Sister Anna. I was capable of running much of the business of the school. Youth has much energy, and I was happy to oblige.

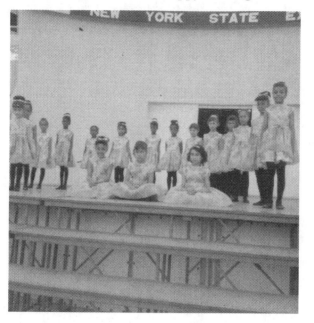

My dancing class

The stories in this book answer the question, "What is it like to be a nun?" This is why I became one. I did not find it difficult to practice my vow of poverty, since I was living with the poor and trying to live like them. My vow of obedience wasn't a problem, since Sister Muriel was so wonderful to all the nuns. She kept us happy with her humorous personality. The pastor of the church would come over to visit us during recreation, and he thoroughly enjoyed our house. He saw that we had much freedom to enable us to work to our fullest potential.

Chastity—that vow was always difficult for me. I did manage to keep it, but it took hard work and much pain. I was always confessing "impure thoughts" in my weekly confession. We worked with the Franciscan Brothers, who taught in the boys' school, and I certainly was attracted to a few of them. The brothers responded in kind. One has to keep in mind that this was an abnormal life that we nuns, brothers, and priests were living. All humans need love, and we were young and looking to be loved. My attraction to one of the brothers was sincere. At one point, he thought that we should leave the religious life. I just could not do that, but just the thought of it made me feel happy and loved. There were many moments when I wondered what I was doing in this type of life. It usually happened at night when I was getting into my bed and feeling lonesome.

Sister Muriel in her wisdom understood this and fostered our friendship with the parish priests and brothers. It was a nice relationship that was present there.

I found that my contact with God was changing and my faith was deepening. Sister Muriel was in charge of the parish school. We did a good job. All of my little first grade boys could read at or above grade level. In the afternoon and after prayers in the evening, we worked with the community. We knew the dangers that lurked in those streets, and we helped the victims of stabbings and beatings. People in the community knew that the convent was a safe place.

I remember there was a wedding in the church that was to be held at three o'clock. The bride waited an hour for the groom, but he did not show. The organist rang our doorbell to tell us the story and that he could not wait any longer. I went over to the church. The bride was in tears. I took her and her party over to the parlor in our convent and tried to calm her down. After I served them tea, someone came over to us and told us the bridegroom was coming. It seemed he was on his way from the Bronx, but they got into some type of bridge accident and could not call. The entire bridge was closed down. These were the days before cell phones. The wedding finally took place—we got someone to play the organ, and all the nuns showed up as well. It was a great ending to a possibly sad situation. I remember the bride never gave up hope and knew he would come. The groom was calm, for he knew she would wait for him. I was amazed at their trust in each other.

The people in the parish would do anything for us. I had a frog named Bozo that the College of Saint Joseph had given to me for my students. His diet consisted of worms. Bozo would eat nothing else. The class started to worry as the supply dwindled. He was in a big glass cage. Actually he would look out at us, and I told my class that he was learning to read with them. I think some of the boys believed it.

One day we had no worms for Bozo. Four of my little boys left the classroom to go to the bathroom. I went to look for them. I saw them through the window of the classroom. This window had a view of all the yards down the entire block. There they were with their mothers, digging for worms. After that, mothers came weekly with worms for Bozo. He lived four more years. As I said, the people of the parish would do anything for us.

One Christmas week, fifteen young black eighth grade girls and I decided to go into Manhattan and see the Rockefeller Center Christmas tree. After that, we wanted some hot chocolate in Schraft's, my then-favorite ice cream place. This was Sister Anna's treat to us. The restaurant was empty, but the waitress told me that there was no room. I could not believe that they would say this to my girls and me. It hit me hard. I told them that I would take two tables and we would stay as long as it took for them to find seating for us. I wanted to show my beautiful girls that they could not accept this in their lives.

We waited in silence. I felt like punching someone. After awhile, I requested to see a manager. The person came and spoke to me. Finally she found us tables. We were seated. This had spoiled the trip for me. How would you feel if this happened to your daughter? I felt as if these were my children and I wanted to cry, but I had to be brave and set a good example.

We were allowed to take our classes on field trips. I selected an animal farm on the North Shore of Long Island. I asked my mother to come along with me to help. She and my sister Teresa and Teresa's little boy, Jimmy, who was three at the time, were along in case of emergency. My class was good, as usual. We had lunch in the picnic area. There were a lot of paper scraps on the ground from classes before us. After we ate, the manager asked me to take my class and leave the park because we had made such a mess of his picnic area.

We had not done this—I, my mother, and my sister were helping the little ones and did not allow any garbage to be on the ground.

Totally angry, my good mother went to the manager and told him we would not leave and that we were going inside to enjoy the park. My class was the best of all the school groups there. All the other schools were white schools.

After we got back on the school bus, my mother asked the bus driver to wait for her. She told me later that she went back inside and told the manager off, and also informed him that she was going to pass the word around to other schools of how he treated us and his mean words to my little ones. Her wish, she told him, was that his business would close down due to this. Believe it or not, my mother did get the word passed to many Catholic schools in Brooklyn. I read a few years later that he closed. It was his mean attitude that hurt.

Five years passed, and Sister Muriel de Lourdes was transferred to another convent. If I remember correctly, she was assigned to be the superior of the rest house in Flushing where Sister Anna lived.

18
Chastity

The replacement for Sister Muriel was Sister Lydia. This unsmiling nun soon succeeded in changing everything that we had been doing for the community. My life began to be strained and hampered by this new superior and her silly rules. At that time, I started to question my life as a nun. The Second Vatican Council had introduced radical changes in the religious life, and I wanted to go along with them. Because of Sister Lydia, I could not.

At this point, we began having more problems with Sister Lydia. She wished to supervise a houseful of nuns whose only tasks were to teach during the day and pray. She strictly forbade contact with the outside world. There were five young nuns in our house who were accustomed to complete interaction with the parish community. As our work continued, Sister Lydia sensed that she was losing control over us. The littlest thing that we did was questioned. For example, I had to get stamps to mail the lunch program requisites. She could not understand why I had to do this. The lunch program from the city required that I send in the milk money by way of a money order. That meant I had to go down to the corner drugstore to procure one. "Why are you doing this to me, and who are you talking to in that drugstore?" she wanted to know. As the time went on and more incidents of this type occurred, we began to realize that she was not too swift. For peace in the convent, the others and I had to plan our actions and be ready with an explanation that would suit her.

Two nuns had the responsibility of taking care of people who had just arrived from Puerto Rico and settled on our shores. Sister Maria was centrally involved in the formation of many prayer groups in the parish church. Sister Nora converted books into Braille for the blind. My charge was to take care of the free lunch program and to put my energy into programs that centered on the black community. There were block associations, track teams, a young mothers' club, and beauty classes for our teenagers, and various other endeavors that we had initiated. I thoroughly relished instructing six-year-old girls in modern interpretive dance. As I stated before, the performances were well received.

Sister Lydia informed us that we must drop our outside activities. This infuriated Sister Nora. She continued her Braille work at night after Sister Lydia was asleep. Sister Maria withdrew into herself and dallied in her cell, reading. The rest of us forged ahead surreptitiously with our work, in spite of the order.

Sister Lydia wanted us out of her way. I often encountered resistance from her when I tried to obtain permission to walk to the corner for the money order or stamps. She accused me of meeting with the brothers and having "intercourse" with them on the way. I assured her that I would return in five minutes and she could watch me from the window. However, her simple mind could not cope with relinquishing authority even for minor details. We had to constantly beg and bargain with her, laughing privately at the absurdity of it.

The Friday afternoon permission was received after bargaining for fifteen minutes. The walk took five minutes. This went on every Friday. I had to pass the house where the priests and brothers lived. I warned them to stay off the street. It became an experience on Fridays as I strolled past the Friary—whistles and cheers and catcalls issued from behind the curtains. I dared not laugh but swallowed hard to keep a straight face. The good brothers helped us do our work in the community, reminding us to keep a sense of humor in all things.

That year on the special feast day of Saint Francis, the good Franciscan Brothers asked Sister Lydia what they could send over to the nuns for the feast. Would manhattans be a good choice? She said, "Yes, but no alcoholic beverages!" The brother came out of her office and knocked on my classroom door to tell me and was stooped over, laughing hysterically.

That evening at supper, Sister Lydia announced that the brothers had sent over manhattans for celebration and that it was to be completely finished by that evening. No celebrations the next day was her order to the twelve of us. I thought I and the other young nuns would choke as we tried to control our laughter. And so as the evening progressed, and Sister Lydia went to bed since she was not into celebrations, we started our drinking. Naturally all of us got looped and fell into our beds that night. In fact, I had to throw the remainder of the drink down the toilet so Sister Lydia would be happy the next day that we had finished the big jar of manhattans.

We had a great friendship with the brothers at the parish. The nuns and brothers interacted with each other every day since the girls' school worked closely with the boys' school. I began to have emotional feelings for one of the young brothers there. I felt it was wrong. He seemed to respond to me in the same way. This went on until he was transferred. During this time, I had a problem with my vow of chastity. I wanted to be loved. When he left I was very sad and did not know how to react. During the following year I was depressed. It was a difficult time in my life.

19
Obedience

On the solemn vow day—called our "Profession Day"—we took the vows of poverty, chastity, and obedience. One of the aspects of obedience was to go wherever we would be sent. Each year, our "Obedience Letter" arrived on the fifteenth of August to every house in the community. I believe there were one hundred twenty-six houses in the community of this order.

The doorbell sounded with a loud gong on that particular August 15th. All the change letters were sent special delivery to arrive on the morning of the infamous day. "From time immemorial," the Holy Rule stated, the letter with all the changes in the entire community should be read exactly at six PM.

Mortification played a major role in a nun's life. The pattern of the change letter typified the suffering we were supposed to endure. The letter was ferried from the deliveryman to its place on the altar in front of the tabernacle. It remained there until six PM. I tried to keep busy all day, but I could not handle this morbid wait. I shook a lot. This special year, I just knew my name was on the list. I told myself maybe—just maybe—it would hold good news. Perhaps Reverend Mother would not pay attention to Sister Lydia and I would be allowed to stay and work for the poor in my beloved Bedford-Stuyvesant. But then my intellect told me this time was my time to move.

With a smile creasing her face, Sister Lydia told us that she had seen Reverend Mother. Reverend Mother agreed that we all needed a rest from our hard work in the poor neighborhoods. We should have more time to devote to our prayer life. This was from a Reverend Mother who I had heard was afraid to come into this neighborhood. Not once did she visit our convent. Sister Lydia's pretext sounded valid. Under her veil was a brain that told her she was not able to keep track of our works. In her own paranoid way, she envisioned us doing all sorts of improper things anathematic with her idea of religious life.

These people I worked with had comprised my family for many years. The six o'clock angelus bell rang. In chapel, we recited the prayer called the *Angelus* as was our daily ritual, then walked in silence, with our hands inside our sleeves, heads bowed, to our places in the dining room. There we stood at attention until the superior said the prayers of "Grace before Meals." After we were seated, she opened the envelope. Naturally Sister had a silver letter opener that glittered. My knees were trembling. Each bone in my body seemed to vibrate.

"Please send Sister Eileen to Holy Name of Mary Convent in Valley Stream to teach the first grade. She shall report there by noon on August 21." I bent my head low. We were forbidden to display any emotion. Our vow of obedience commanded that we serve blindly. Emotionally and spiritually numb, I could not demonstrate even if I wanted to, for I was immersed in anger. She had every one of us transferred to different convents. I tried to understand God's design for me—that was *supposed* to be uppermost in my mind.

I had been taught to reverence a Power
That is the visible quality and shape
And image of right reason: that matures
Her processes by steadfast laws; gives birth
To no impatient or fallacious hopes,
No heat of passion or excessive zeal,
No vain conceits; provokes to no quick turns
Of self-applauding intellect; but rains
To meekness, and exalts by humble faith.

—*Wordsworth*

Perhaps I had simply overlooked the presence of politics in the convent. There was no recourse. I could not appeal to any authoritative body. Although I desperately wanted to remain in Bedford-Stuyvesant, I had to obey the order that would take me away from my friends and those in need. My disenchantment leaped forward, and suddenly a thought wormed its way into my anger and frustration and depression—politics and money play a large role in organizations.

We went directly to night prayers in the chapel for one-half hour. I maintained my cool composure throughout the prayers. Sacred Silence was offered. I presume Sister Lydia did this purposely so as to avoid any scenes. We all adjourned to our rooms. As I climbed the dilapidated wooden stairs, my eyes burned. I entered the door of my cell and slammed it behind me. This little room had only a bed, bureau, and a small table and lamp. I drew down the shades to ward off the glare of the streetlights. For practical reasons, I would not cry. The other nuns would hear me. They also had to move to other faraway places. We had to be strong for each other.

I wrenched off my long black habit and the starched headpiece. Instead of folding my veil into eighths and tucking it between two heavy pieces of cardboard to insert beneath my mattress to keep it pressed nicely, I tossed it on the bare wooden floor. I sprawled on the hard bed and felt violently sick. The order to send me to a wealthy convent in suburbia was too obvious. The people at the top were certainly out of touch with reality. Bedford-Stuyvesant was as real and immediate as one could get. I was needed here. The church was needed here. The church is not a beautiful marble building in the midst of tenement dwellings. The church is people working together to help each other.

I also felt that the hurt was to the good people of the parish and really believed that God was agreeing with me. When the parish people heard that we were transferred, they gave us a big block party and cried as we said our good-byes.

On the morning of August 21ˢᵗ, our families came to take us to our new assignments. I had to be strong for my family. When I arrived at my new home, the building was new and beautifully furnished. It was quite different from the convents that I was used to living in. I went to bed that night in a lovely room, with a nice bed, desk, lamp, my own bathroom, and other amenities that I had not been used to. *I will get used to it*, I thought, as I fell exhausted into a deep sleep.

I stayed in this convent for one year. It was pleasant enough. I taught first grade in the school. The students were from upper-middle-class families. The parents were helpful with anything that we wished to do in the school.

My charge in this convent was to take care of the accounting books and to also help the superior. She was younger than most and, therefore, I just had to make her bed and clean her room in the morning before school.

I was amazed at the money this place had on the books. I had to go to a training class in the motherhouse to learn how to carefully keep the books. I majored in accounting in college, and thus they picked me for the job. I did not like it—it was boring—but I learned that each convent was independent. The pastor paid the salaries of the nuns, and he was able to be generous due to the contributions of the wealthy parishioners. Sister told me to order curtains for the entire convent. We already had three sets. However, Sister said we had to use the money. The convent was taxed by the motherhouse. She wanted to use up some of the excess money. I felt this was so against the order of things. Here was our convent in the poor neighborhood struggling, having not even one set of curtains until I sewed them, and now I would have to order more sets for this place. We had fruit on the table daily, and anything you wished was available to you. I found this difficult to understand.

I made it known to Reverend Mother that *I* wished to work with the poor.

20
My Summer

The congregation of nuns I joined was founded primarily to teach in elementary and secondary schools, and at the college level. There were also several hospitals that were run by the order. I yearned to continue my work with the poor. That summer I was happy to be chosen with one other nun to work in a help center for the poor in Oceanhill-Brownsville. We were told by our superior that the order trusted us to go out into the world to work. I felt that this was where I was most needed. During that summer I was amazed how my life had dramatically changed.

Sister and I worked out of Presentation Church on Eastern Parkway. We lived in the convent attached to Bishop McDonnell High School further down on Eastern Parkway. Three days a week, we assembled about five hundred little children from the streets and took them to Coney Island for the day. We divided them into groups of ten, and gave each child a special color tag to wear that matched the tag of the group leader. Each teenaged group leader was hired by the City of New York under a youth job program. The work they performed was programmed by sister and me.

It was a sight to behold, walking five hundred strong down the subway and holding open the doors until all the children were on board. I walked the beach supervising and would have loved to have taken off my heavy black serge habit and hot starch hat and veil and jump into the water. One day, as we were rounding up the little ones, I had a four-year-old by the hand. As we started off toward the train, I heard, "Hey, Sis, you can give me back my child now. He is not with your group." This little child had stayed by my side the entire day. I thought he was in our group and had lost his ticket. His mother said that he liked nuns.

Jobs were very scarce for young black men. I believed then, and I still believe, that this is the answer to many of the woes of society today—jobs, to get people out of poverty and feeling good about themselves. I succeeded in getting one job for a young person. I went to his tenement house and called for him to come down, that I had a job for him. As soon as I said "job," a door opened on the first floor, and there appeared about six tall young black men, all saying to me, "Sis, could you get us a job also?" I told them that I would try. We had an office in the rectory that I worked out of. My sister Marjorie worked in the city for Asiatic Oil. She succeeded in placing one of our young ladies in her company, but I was unable to obtain jobs for the men. It was so sad for those nice young men.

One very hot 98-degree day in the summer, I was crossing Eastern Parkway by Presentation Church. We had a building called the Center down the block from where we worked. A car stopped, and a man rolled down his window to speak to me. He hollered at me, "Hey, Sister, see those open hydrants—I am disgusted. I just spent five hundred dollars on a new lawn, and I cannot water it. It will die. But all these people can use this water. They have water, and I don't." I looked at him and felt sorry for him and his anger. All I could say was, "These small children are dying in the heat of the city and have no air-conditioning or pools. They really need to have water sprinklers to survive in this hot place." Off he went, angry with me. Life gets tough at times.

When I was transferred to Valley Stream, I collected clothes for the Center in Presentation Parish in Oceanhill-Brownsville. I knew the priests and people working there would be happy to distribute them to the needy. I also wished for the students in Valley Stream to witness how they could help others. The kids were great. We placed the cartons into a school bus, and I asked my superior if I could lead in the convent station wagon. At first, she was hesitant, having the car go into such a poor neighborhood. Finally she relented. I took the convent station wagon and drove to the Center. The bus followed. We parked outside the large building. When I came out, one tire and four hubcaps were missing. Oh, oh, my superior was going to be angry. There were a bunch of young guys sitting nearby, and I complained to them. They asked, "Sis, is that your station wagon?" I said, "Yes." The guys said, "Wait a minute." In a few minutes, the tire and hubcaps were back on the car, and off I went, home to suburbia.

Sister and I worked in this parish in Oceanhill-Brownsville for the entire summer. I lived in a nearby convent and had to take a bus home. We spent our days trying to get jobs for people, going to Coney Island with the children, and teaching remedial classes at the Center. Every day was a new challenge. However, many days were so full that I was always running up the street to catch the bus to be home by supper at 6:00 PM. One day, as I was running up the block, I missed the bus. It pulled away. I stopped and said to myself, *now what?* There were eight young black men standing on the corner. "Is that the bus you were running for?" they called. I said, "Yes." I watched in amazement as they joined hands in front of the bus and made it stop. Then the guys told the bus to wait for me, and I came onto the bus. The people just looked at me strangely. This happened so many times that the bus driver knew enough to wait for me on days that I was not waiting on the corner.

At the end of a long, hot, dirty day, all twelve project workers gathered around an altar in an upper room of the Center. The workers in this poverty program project were volunteers. There were several young men who were in training to become priests, a few others who were in training to be religious brothers, and several girls who were training to be nuns like ourselves from different orders. We all were donating our summer to work here in the center of Our Lady of the Presentation to assist the priest who was stationed there, as he helped the poor.

In that upper room of the Center, one of the priests offered Mass for us, and we prayed for all the people we served. What an inspiration it was for me! It reminded me of Christ's appearance in the upper room at the first Pentecost after his resurrection from the tomb.

On weekends, I had to go back to Valley Stream, where I would regale the nuns with the stories of what I did during the week. They had never heard of such goings-on.

21
New Assignment

September arrived. I was reassigned to teach further out on Long Island in a middle-class neighborhood. It was clear that they were not going to let me work with the poor. I knew it was up to me to take matters into my own hands. Sister Anna had taught me that important lesson.

I became very unhappy with the way that I was living my life. I approached Reverend Mother and told her of my unhappiness. She listened to me and said nothing. After that, I made an appointment to see Sister Antonella, my former Mistress of Novices. I shared with her my frustrations and my desire to work with the poor. Sister Antonella, that saintly woman, told me not to be afraid to leave the order, since she knew that they would never allow me to work with the poor again. It was in the plans of the order to have schools only in wealthier places, which would bring in money to the motherhouse. The future plan for the order was to close all the convents in Bedford-Stuyvesant.

When Reverend Mother found out that I had spoken to Sister Antonella, she was quite angry. As the school year ended in June, I was ordered to present myself at the motherhouse to keep an appointment with Reverend Mother, and was told to be prepared to stay for the entire summer. I was quite nervous about this new development. To be ordered to meet with Reverend Mother was a very serious situation.

One of the nuns in my convent drove me over to the grounds of the motherhouse, which consisted of numerous acres of land. As she let me out and started to drive away through those large black gates, she hollered, "Good Luck."

I started to shake and began the long walk and climb up to the second floor where Reverend Mother had her offices. I was told to sit outside her office until her secretary came out. I waited one half hour sitting on those hard chairs. I had not eaten any breakfast and my stomach was growling. The sweat was running down under my arms and the palms of my hands were really dripping from nervousness.

Finally I was motioned inside to a large, grand office the size of a small ballroom. It was richly furnished—not what I was used to while living in the poor missions of Brooklyn. I was told to kneel down, as was the custom when speaking to Reverend Mother. You always did that on your knees, with eyes down and arms in your sleeves.

I heard, "Dear Sister, you are being assigned to the former priest's house on the northern part of these grounds where you will spend the summer. It is empty now and you will live in that house with several young nuns who are working in the nearby parish. I am instructing you not to leave this house, or have any visitors. Once a day you may take a walk to the cemetery which is a mile up the road. In September you will go back to teach in West Islip. That is all. You may go."

I got up and nearly tripped on my skirt. I walked out in a daze. *She does not want other nuns to hear of her plans, I figured. That is so unfair not to be honest.*

I had some serious thinking to do during this time. I returned to West Islip and continued to teach first grade. However, as the year progressed, I was overcome with sadness.

The type of living has left you
Tired, unloved, and weary
Now you realize you were never meant to
climb that mountain

                              —*Anonymous*

22
I Had to Leave

I sat behind the wheel of the convent station wagon, staring at the long road before me. I was exhausted from the stress of my problem. Here I was, Eileen the nun, about to tell my sister Margie that I was doing the inconceivable—leaving the cloistered life of a nun in a convent and coming back out into the world to live. I would need her help.

From the main road, I went down several country lanes until her lovely home came into view. The children were playing on the front lawn. I knew she was home, because her BMW was parked in the driveway. My heart began to beat faster at the thought of what I was about to put into motion. Suddenly the thought came to me that perhaps I should not do this. I can still feel the fear that felled my body at that moment.

The children came running over to the car as I parked it in the driveway. "Oh, hello, Aunt Eileen," they shouted. I looked at them and smiled as I got out of the car. My sister came to the side door, waving me inside. *This is it*, I decided. Giving the kids a big hug, I went inside. Over a cup of tea, I told Margie of my plan and asked for her help. She thought a minute, looked at me, and with a very stern face, said, "Go back to the convent and do as they say. I cannot help you."

Outside the sun was shining, but in this moment of time, I truly crashed into a most dark circle. Margie was staring at me. She was very concerned about our parents. This act of mine would be the ultimate disappointment for them in their retirement years. Margie said she had to take the children to a game and left me in her house, all alone. I cried and sobbed uncontrollably for a long time.

By 4:30, I pulled myself together, closed her door, and got into the car. It seemed to me that my life was to depend on what others wanted me to do. I did not understand why I couldn't get help from my family. Certainly I would reach out to them if they needed me. Driving toward the highway, I knew that this less-traveled road was one that I must go alone.

My daily living in the convent was becoming a crucifixion with no resurrection in sight. I had to leave. It was painful to do so—after all, I had selected this life. Where would I get the strength to leave it? After seventeen years, what could I do? Where could I go? I needed money, a place to live, clothes, and a job. Would I be able to do this? There was not one person in the entire world that I could turn to at this time.

My body was bone-thin. Depression had taken hold of me. All there was in my possession were a long, black habit, black nun's shoes, and a shaven head. What in heaven's name was I to do? The other nuns in the convent sensed what was up. Everyone around moved away when they saw me coming. It was considered a terrible deed to leave the order. Here I was, one of their popular, hardworking, creative nuns, thinking of doing just that.

Very little energy was left in my body. I did not care that the other nuns treated me like a leper. Just as well. It was difficult enough to plan how I was to leave, and I did not wish to be pressed into conversation. Sister Alma, the nun who sponsored me, heard the rumors. She took the train from Brooklyn and a cab to see me. Upon arrival at my convent on Long Island, we went into the parlor and closed the door. Sister said, "I think that you should know that I have heard these horrible rumors about what you are thinking of doing. My advice to you is do not embarrass us by what you are about to do. Your family and I are very disappointed in you." Then, amid this confusion, she called a cab and left.

I lay awake in my cell, knowing that my family now knew of my decision. I assume Margie told Teresa and Teresa told my mom and dad. Their dream of having a daughter as a nun, someone who would be their key into heaven, came crumbling down. Their family would be held up to ridicule from the relatives and neighbors, and their proud name probably would be destroyed—or so they thought.

Early in March, I asked permission to use the convent station wagon for my personal use for the day. The rule had just been changed, and now we were allowed to get the car for our private errands. No one was to know where I was going. I had to get away from people—far away. I wanted to escape to no-man's-land. I slipped the car into drive and headed to the solitary ocean at Montauk Point. Very few people would be there at this time of the year. Driving through the small towns was an entirely new experience for me. Now and then, someone would wave to me. I waved back. I needed gas. Also, I had to use the bathroom. Where could I go without causing a commotion? We were instructed never to use public facilities for the same reason of not appearing human. I got up courage—which seems awfully silly now—to ask the man at the station for the key. Even little things like this were difficult for me. I had never been allowed to do any of these things before. It was like an alien coming down to earth and hiding in a nun's habit.

I traveled through the quaint towns of Westhampton, Quogue, Hampton Bays, Southampton, Bridgehampton, East Hampton, Amagansett, and onward. After many miles, I saw the sign saying "MONTAUK This Way." I passed Panorama and Guerney's and went through the town of Montauk. I wanted to stop for a soda, but I did not have the courage to get out of the car and face people. There in the distance loomed the Montauk lighthouse and the wild ocean. I parked in the lonely lighthouse parking lot. The day was overcast and dreary. Only one other car was there.

Looking around, I saw cliffs to my right. Deciding it would be fun to climb up the cliffs, I pulled up my skirt and headed to the top of the highest one. It was exciting to look down at the powerful ocean. I sat down on the ground and felt all alone in the world. My first thoughts as I stared at the pounding surf had been that I simply wanted to live my own life. My heart was pounding, and I was trembling at the decision I was about to make. Seriously I struggled to throw it out of my head, as if this was some sort of a dream. What a perilous moment this was for me. The wind was blowing my black veil off my head. The ocean lay very still as far out as one could see.

Peace came suddenly. Here I was so scared, heart pounding, and out there all was calm. Was this the way God was assuring me that all would turn out fine?

The words by Anne Morrow Lindbergh in *Gift from the Sea* came back to me.

> *But there are*
> *other beaches to explore. There*
> *are more shells to find. This*
> *is only a beginning.*

My life was like the tide. At times forceful—at other times weak. I thought, *There is so much more in life than this one as a nun. There is a whole lot of living I still have to do. I must not waste it. I do not have to die to myself. I can live, love, and be happy, and spread God's love in a real way.* It was possible. I would do it.

On that bleak, windy day in late March, sitting on a high cliff overlooking the Atlantic Ocean, with the foghorn warning small craft and the gulls flying around very free, I made up my mind. I planned that day how to leave the convent and make my dreams a reality!

I picked my way down the rocky cliffs, literally running and jumping with joy—my veil was blowing and nearly flew off. I tripped and fell but didn't care. I praised God for my life. I was singing "Climb Every Mountain" over and over again.

After I got into the car, I turned on the radio, rev'd the engine, and started down the road, the only car in sight. At this point, the highway winds up and down over the hills, with the ocean on all sides. This road was leading me into town and back to civilization. It seemed to be a starting point for my new life, all fresh and exciting and good. I wanted to shout the good news to the whole world.

There was a little country church off to the side of the road, standing alone, small and holy, with the steeple pointing to the sky. There it stood—so silent, so strong, and so alone. I felt I belonged to it. The quiet surrounded us. I stopped the car and eased out, being careful not to break the silence.

As I entered the tiny chapel, I saw the sun's glow streaming through the stained-glass windows. It was a quaint old wooden church with about sixty pews. I walked toward the tabernacle. There was a flicker of a candle nearby. I knelt in front of it in humble adoration. The spiritual allure of the candle added to my feelings of closeness to God. I praised him and thanked him for giving me the courage to see things clearly. I know he loves me more than I can ever imagine. I love my own father very much. He is a good person and a wonderful father. Meditating on this has helped me realize a little about perfect love, a divine mystery I cannot fully understand. I knew then that I would continue to grow spiritually outside the cloister. Leaving the little church, I noticed the ocean before me. Its' swells pounding on the sand were powerful and constant, reminding me of the swells pounding in my chest, up and down, pounding and consistent and sure.

When I returned to the convent, I found a phone message that my sister Teresa had called. I called her back. It seems that Margie had told her of my unhappiness and possible leaving. Teresa begged me not to say anything about my problem for the next three months. "Mom will be too upset. Maybe in a few months' time, you will see things clearly. We all get upset. I will pray for you." I told her my mind was made up, but I would wait awhile before telling my parents. I could not promise three months of silence about my decision.

Since she lived downstairs from my parents, her family would have to bear the brunt of the forthcoming anger and unsettlement. Nothing I could do would help her in this situation. I felt sorry for her. I knew the times ahead would be rough in that house. I had told Margie first, for we were always close; as the oldest, Teresa would try to talk me out of it. However, neither of my sisters grasped my predicament, so they could not help my parents to see why I had to do this hideous thing.

In going through these various changes, I inevitably hurt people, or at least made them uncomfortable. They were so used to boxing me in that when I decided to "get out of the box," they became upset. And so did I. Teresa contacted many family friends who were religious. She asked them to convince me to remain in the convent. I felt this would happen, so I was prepared.

One day in May, I was cleaning and waxing the long corridor by the bedrooms. The front doorbell rang. Since I was the only one home at the time, I fixed myself up to look presentable and went to open the front door. It was Monsignor Whelan, all the way from Brooklyn to counsel me. "Hi, Monsignor, come in." He put his arms around me, gave me a big hug, and said, "Poor Eileen, you are so mixed up—I will help you." A gentle person, he had been my dearest friend since I was ten years old. I cared for him a lot. But here he was, trying to tell me to stay, hardly aware of my suffering. By then, I had no intention of changing my mind and just needed help to achieve my goal.

As I grew angry, Monsignor confronted me with tears in his eyes. "I have heard the terrible news. God wants you here—you know that. You made promises and cannot break these promises without breaking God's heart." I tried to interject that I had taken all of these things into consideration. Monsignor clasped my hands and pleaded. "Your leaving means giving bad example to all the young nuns that you teach in college."

During the past year I was assigned as an instructor in the order's college. The goal of the college was to instruct young nuns in methods of teaching. I was assigned to teach classes for several semesters in reading, math, and religion.

"It means turning your back on all the future children of God that you are supposed to instruct. Now there will be a void in their lives." His voice boomed, emphatic. "The devil is telling you that it is better on the outside. It is not. In fact, it is awful, and you will end up in a terrible state. Eileen, you have to stop these thoughts—you must stay!"

I cried, and waved an arm toward the door. "Monsignor, please leave." He rose, clearly distraught. I wanted him to help, but he was not capable of understanding my pain. "Monsignor, I need help. If you cannot help me, then I wish you would not come again." He responded, "Eileen, I will not be coming again. I will pray for your soul. God help you." We quickly exchanged good-byes.

A little while later, all the nuns returned. The prayer bell rang. We marched to chapel. No, I did not cry. Anger welled up in my bones, rage at his nonsense. I thought he was intelligent. He turned out to be like so many others—not understanding at all what I was going through. The days passed. Teresa was doing a good job. Father Burke arrived. "Everyone looks up to you, and you have a responsibility to keep this image. Think of the faith of others. You will shake it and will have to answer to God for it. You will kill your mother. Just put the thought out of your head. Then laugh. Laugh and laugh. Everything will be fine." He then got up and started to leave. I said good-bye to him and closed the door.

The newspaper, *Newsday* wanted to publish an article about nuns, religion, and children. The Diocese gave the newspaper staff permission to interview me since I had just started an interesting and very successful parent educator program (PEP) in religion in a parish located in West Islip.

This did not make me very happy, since I was planning to leave the convent in the very near future. Of course, the priests of the Diocese did not know of my decision to leave. On the day of the interview, a young lady reporter arrived with a camera crew. When the interview was over, I confided with the reporter that I planned to leave the convent. She wrote the article and reported all that I told her back to her boss. A few days later, she telephoned me to say that when I leave the convent, there would be a job waiting for me at *Newsday*, and that all I had to do was sign in at the personnel office. So now I had a job to go to.

Everyone was trying to dissuade me from leaving the convent. That is exactly why I came to my decision before telling my family. I loved them and was quite aware of the terrible hurt they would feel. To leave the convent in those days was a terrible disgrace. We had professed perpetual vows to God. And God, they figured, would be angry. But I knew a God of soft humanity and complete understanding.

One day during this time, I went home to Brooklyn for a visit. Home was a two-story brownstone in Windsor Terrace. My sister, as I have mentioned before, lived on the first floor with her family, and my mother and father resided in the apartment upstairs. As I climbed the stairs, I saw my mother in the kitchen preparing the meal. Whenever I planned to come home, my mom would prepare a really delicious meal for me. This day it was steak, french-fried potatoes, and fresh vegetables. Nothing was too good for a religious nun, especially her daughter.

After kissing my mother hello, I walked down the hall to the living room. My father was nursing a cocktail and watching the news on the television. As soon as I entered the room, he stood and plumped the pillows in my mother's comfortable chair and told me to sit there. He switched off the TV. My father certainly would be able to help me and offer me advice. I sat down close to him on the couch. Softly I whispered that I had something very important to tell him, but he could not tell my mom. I believed he thought I was pregnant. He did seem relieved when he heard my story. "Oh, is that all you want to do?" he asked. I felt a load lifted off my shoulders. However, he told me my mother would never accept it and I would probably not be welcome back into the house. His face wrinkled up, and he seemed so old at this point. "Where will you live, where can you find a job, and at your age, what can you do?" he asked.

At that moment, my mother called us to supper. My father told me not to dare tell my mother. We strolled into the dining room. At the large table that was dressed with an Irish linen tablecloth and napkins, flowers, and the best Waterford crystal, I felt sad.

My mother was always happy to serve me. It was awful to have to cause this suffering after the years she had devoted to me in the convent. I presume my face showed it. My father studied me, puzzled. After the meal, I helped my mother clean up, and as was their custom, we walked into the living room to watch the six-o'clock news on television. At seven o'clock, I had to leave. I kissed them good-bye. Not another word was said. I told my sister and her family that I was going. They all kissed me good-bye. I left and drove back to the convent, happy that I had the opportunity to have unburdened myself to my father.

Maybe he thought it was a dream that would disappear. Of course, he never liked nuns and did not want me to become one. He used to say funny things about nuns and told jokes about them. He considered their lives outdated. I was his favorite daughter. I think he was happy to rescue me.

My father's religious philosophy was less stern than my mother's. She adhered strictly to the rules. He enjoyed life more and did not bother with many of the regulations. Oh, he was a devoted Catholic, but he was more realistic about life and the church. My parents lived their religious lives separately, even to the point of walking by themselves to church each morning for Mass. My father walked faster than my mother, so he gave her a ten-minute head start. They sat on opposite sides, as was customary for many couples in those days.

Time was going by. My mother had to be told. No one wanted to do it, and no one wanted me to tell her. My concern was that one of her many nun friends would surmise and mention it to her. My mother was so proud of her daughter, the nun. In our neighborhood, when you met someone with a child in religion, the greeting usually followed, "And how is your daughter Eileen?" That opened the topic of where I was stationed and my good works.

My mother and Teresa and her children were going to spend the weekend with Margie in the country. I drove over from the convent, determined to break the news. My sisters were inspecting flowers in the garden. I climbed out of the car. Trembling, I walked up to them, and they knew. They became angry and fearful. Teresa said, "How can you do this—Mom will die of a heart attack." Little did they realize I myself was in a terrible state. But I could only think of my mother hearing it from someone else. My sisters announced they were going to stroll down the road, away from the house.

Once in the lovely large kitchen, I faced my good mom, peeling potatoes at the sink for the evening meal. I kissed her and sat down at the kitchen table. Shaking, I said, "Mom, I have been very unhappy for a long time now. I think if I had a year away from the convent, it would help me. I have decided to take a year's leave of absence." My mother froze. I thought, *Oh, God, let her take this calmly.* She didn't move, didn't say a word. As I stammered, my mother cut me off. "Please leave."

My eyes burned with tears, but I held them in as I rose. My mother said that she did not wish to see me again. My sisters had disappeared down the road. Their plan from now on was to run away. I said that I was too upset to stay. I walked out the door as my mother continued to peel potatoes. It tore her apart, I know, but at that moment my heart was broken, too. I did not get angry. I did not hate. I now was a listless nonperson, wallowing in sorrow.

They cut off all ties with me, completely ignoring me as if I were a criminal. It was their way of saying, "Get back in the convent." I called my sisters, and they were cold or busy. I was instructed not to call my mother. My father remained on the sidelines. My mother figured if everyone ignored me, I'd reconsider. At least, that was the way I interpreted the picture. My parents were very generous to both of my sisters and their families. A friend of the family told me years later that my sisters felt indebted to my parents and followed my mother's orders in this instance. I had to accept this stance that my family took.

There was a big problem that I had to solve. If I planned to work and live on Long Island, a car was a necessity. I requested a loan of four hundred dollars from my parents and assured them I would pay it back shortly. My parents adamantly stated they would certainly not think of such a thing. They told me not to come home again until I decided to stay in the convent. A priest I knew had offered to loan me money for the car, so I really was not worried. But I wished they would help me. Crying hysterically, I screamed that I didn't need the money, but I did need their love and concern. In the end, my father came out with me to buy a Volkswagen. Then he left. I was completely alone and apart. Where was God?

Next, I needed a place to send my trunk and a mailing address. I tried to ask Margie for it. I called her. She said her basement was too damp, and wondered why in the world would I use her house for a forwarding address, since I certainly had no intention of living there—did I?

I will never forget these events. I was frightened. Leaving was certainly difficult, my family was not going to help or bother with me, I had no place to go, no clothes, no job, no friends—what was I to do? I prayed to God constantly, pleading with him for assistance.

It was my one consolation—knowing I had him on my side. He was walking beside me.

Ah, my dear God! Though I am
clean forgot,
Let me not love me, if I love
Thee not.

Reverend Mother had heard rumors that I was probably considering leaving. I suppose my personality change was obvious to all. The hierarchy ignored my situation and offered no help. I was surprised. After seventeen years of working so hard and diligently for the community, I was receiving the silent treatment. A friend of mine, Maura, was also a nun in another order. After we both left the convent, she told me that her order had sent her for counseling and helped her set up in an apartment at Columbia University, where she was able to get a fellowship. They also kept in touch to make sure that she was okay. However, I had become so disillusioned that I really hadn't expected anything from my order of nuns. Because meals were conducted in silence, and because we had to be silent and proper nuns, we should really be silent about our emotions, too. The silence in the convent rooms and corridors was bothering me.

Probably no one wished to be near me. I presume they thought I was a bad person, filled with the devil, to want to leave and go out "into the dreadful world outside." Hadn't we beaten ourselves with chains every Saturday night as if to compensate for all the evil people enjoying themselves?

I had been working with several priests in the diocese on religious education for children. One of my dear friends, Father Schaefer, called me on the phone, which was in an open hallway so everyone could hear what was said. He tried so hard to comfort me, and had me laughing when he told me to hang on with my fingernails, because when all this was over and there were no nuns left, the property would be split up and I would be rich. Smiling, I told him that I could not wait that long.

With stiffened spine, I searched for courage. I remember my father saying how strong I was. I did not want to be that strong. Sometimes, when I look back, I suspect I cried the summer away.

My tears, however, were not the idle tears of self-pity. I saw my life wasted—doing nothing in a world that needs enormous help. My tears were for the tears and tribulations of my friends in the ghetto. They are misunderstood also. I expected much more from the holy life.

Most of the sisters had summer assignments. I did not receive one, due to the fact they expected me to depart in June. I was living alone in a twelve-bedroom convent, about to be closed for the summer. I contacted the publishing company about the book I had written on parent education. I explained the situation. The editors there suggested I complete the manuscript immediately. They rushed it, thus allowing me some money. My strength seeped back into my bones. There was now an order I could follow. The publishing company advised me to come into their office when I did leave, and they would give me an advance to help me out. I then planned to leave in August. I needed a job.

There is a time for grieving ...
A time for sorrowing ...
A time for courage ...

Four weeks later, I finished the manuscript and mailed it to the publishing company. During the past two years, I had often lectured around Brooklyn and Long Island, handing in my honoraria to the superior. After my last speech, I decided to keep the money for myself, the grand sum of eighty dollars. I placed it in a bank account in my secular name, in Garden City. I packed my trunk. I stole two new blankets from the convent storage room, and four sheets. I would need them, for they were all I had in this world. At least I would sleep at night wherever I would be. I closed and locked my trunk.

I put no mailing label on the trunk because I didn't know where I was going and where I would end up. My plan was to return someday and take care of the trunk labeling problem. At the moment, I had enough to worry about.

I was really running scared. The thought was in my mind that I might not be able to support myself or survive in the outside world. Perhaps I would have to go back into the convent.

Of course, it didn't help matters any when the old priest in his homily, at a Sunday Mass attended by my parents, pounded the lectern and shouted, "Any nun who leaves the convent will end up in hell!" I definitely could not go home to my parents after that.

Again I realized that my sister Teresa and her husband Tom, with their children Therese, Jimmy, and Sara, were bearing the brunt of what I was doing. I could do nothing to help that situation.

23
Angels to Help Me

I stayed in the empty convent building despairing through the month of July. I spoke to no one. The phones were turned off, and I had enough food in the convent freezer to keep me going.

In early August, I applied for and received permission from the motherhouse to go on my yearly solitary retreat. This year all nuns were allowed to choose their own place for the solitary retreat. Before this year, we all had to attend our yearly retreat on the motherhouse grounds and chapel.

I planned to go as far away from the motherhouse as I could and picked a monastery in Newton, New Jersey. I knew in my heart that I would not be returning to the convent, but I just had to get up the courage to walk out the door one last time and walk down that long road into the unknown. To me, that was very scary.

I told the monk in charge of my retreat of my plans to leave the convent, and he strongly discouraged me. He had to go away for a few days and said when he came back, he expected me to come to my senses.

He left me alone in this huge retreat house, nearly empty except for an elderly couple. The monks lived across the road in their monastery. I was scared and didn't sleep at all that first night. The next morning, I walked to the monastery for breakfast, where I met the couple, who were friends of the head monk. I felt good knowing that I was not alone in that building.

They took a liking to me and asked the head monk for permission to take me out for dinner. Because I did not want to deceive them, I told them of my plans to leave. Imagine my surprise when they told me they were the owners of a women's designer clothing store on Long Island. Both of them got excited, planning to outfit me with the best clothes for my future life. Nellie gave me a few outfits that they happened to have in the trunk of their car and told me to come visit them after two weeks for the rest of my wardrobe. If I did not, they said they would be hurt and insulted. I promised.

I stayed at the retreat house for one week. God was on my side. The next morning, I opened the front door of the retreat house. The sun was just rising. Because I did not want to arouse suspicion, I wore my habit. I had my other outfits in a suitcase. The bus arrived. I stepped up and paid my ticket to the Port Authority and sat down. I had accomplished this horrendous feat. My body was shaking, and my face and hands were sweating. My only thought was, *Oh, God, what have I done?*

I never went back to the convent. I just walked off the bus and into an unknown world. My life as a homeless person was about to begin.

24
Removing the Habit

The Port Authority bus terminal was huge, with people everywhere rushing and bumping into me. I was frozen. A few people came over and gave me quarters, thinking I was a begging nun.

I grew up in the city. I knew how to get around. Besides, in my pocket was eighty dollars that I had received when I gave a speech about religious education. Remember, I had not turned it in. I felt rich.

It was a treat to go to McDonald's for lunch. After that, I walked down Eighth Avenue and decided to take in a movie. I had not seen one in seventeen years. I could rest in there. The second I sat down, a strange woman sat next to me and leaned over and pressed her arm against mine. I said nothing, froze, and then jumped up and moved to the other side of the movie house.

I was alone and had to be careful. For supper, there was McDonald's again. That night I went to another movie house that was open all night. I washed in the ladies' room. I took off my habit and put on one of the outfits from Nellie and my trusted Capezios. The shoes were back in style. I smiled.

The following day, I had to make plans. I went to Penn Station and slept in the waiting room. I remembered a girl I went to school with, and I knew her mother lived in a large house on Long Island. I had to get a place to live and a job. I called the number I found in the phone book and asked if I could rent a room upstairs for a while. She said, "Yes, dear, come and live with me for a little while until you get settled. I have a large room and bath upstairs. You can have it. And the rent will help me a lot."

I needed something to eat and went to my "happy hunting ground" behind the grocery store and found apples, grapes, and pears. That would suffice for a while.

I took the train and arrived at her house in good time. She was a nurse and worked nights, so I had the place to myself.

My parents decided to help me out by buying me a small Volkswagon. That allowed me to look for a teaching position on Long Island. When my father came with me to purchase the car, we parked it behind the convent in West Islip.

My friend came out to visit her mother, and we drove out to get my car so I could start looking for a job. I needed to support myself. I called the convent that evening with instructions on where to send my trunk.

My hair needed to be cut. That would be an interesting trip, since I had never gone to a beauty parlor before. Plus, my Capezio's were now worn out. I had begun my journey seventeen long years before with them as a safety valve. Now that they had done their job, it was time for a new pair of shoes.

25
After Leaving the Convent

There was a lot on my plate. Now at least I had a job and a place to live. It was a typical Levittown house with one large room and bath on the second floor. It had a big bed. This was all I needed.

The lady who owned the house was kind. Mary was her daughter and she came to see me that weekend and we went clothes shopping. The little orange dress was not a good purchase. Mary helped me shop for casual items. She also helped me look up the classified ads for a position in teaching. I made a few phone calls and received an invite to go to a nursery school in Woodbury for an interview.

Mary left to go back to the city. Her mother worked nights in the local hospital. Here I was, all alone in the room on the second floor. Not bad, I thought. I could peek out the window and watch the world go by. I sat downstairs and watched TV in her mother's living room. Watching TV was a new experience for me, and I truly enjoyed every moment.

About eight o'clock that night, I felt brave and left the house. I walked to the local shopping mall and found a pizza store. I bought a small slice of pizza and brought it back to the house. That pizza slice was the first one I had since I was seventeen years old and it tasted great. Mary's mother was expected home around midnight. I did not want to speak to her so I ran upstairs and made believe I was asleep when she came up to check on me. It was my shyness that was holding me back.

The next morning was Monday. I called *Newsday* and said that I would be reporting for the library position that was offered to me. I was really scared. When I arrived the people I met were extremely gracious. They showed me how to research information for the reporters, writers, and editors. Word got around the newspaper staff that I had just left the convent. This was big news back in those days. Many people started to come down to my desk and look me over. After several days of that, it got to be too much and I made a decision that teaching would be easier for me.

On my first day of work at *Newsday* I had to fill out my W-2 form for income tax purposes using my parent's address. When the vice president saw it, he sent for me. I sat across from him at his large desk. He looked at me, and said, "Do you know who I am?" I said, "No." He continued, "I am the little Jewish boy who lived across the street from you when we were growing up." It was Stan Asimov. I could not believe it.

Stan had given me my first job at *Newsday* and wanted me to attend Columbia School of Journalism. He said that he would enroll me and show me how to obtain my journalism degree. I was too nervous at the time to try anything. Teaching would be where I would feel more comfortable.

I did leave *Newsday* after working there for about one week, but Stan Asimov was a dear friend until his death a few years ago. I will always be grateful to him for all his help and encouragement.

While on retreat, I had written a letter to the convent informing them I was leaving and would not be coming back. I also had written a letter to my family telling them the same thing. I gave them this address. As I said before, my father had bought me a little car the month before. He knew I would need it to look for a job. I realized that the car was from both my mom and dad. That was a big gift and help for me in starting my new life. I will never forget their kindness, even though they were very upset and worried about me.

The next morning I awoke to the call from Mary's mother to get dressed and come downstairs to meet someone. I did and was introduced to the high school principal who had just been divorced.

He wanted to ask me out on a date. I said thanks, but I was not ready. I found my way upstairs and proceeded to break out in hives. What in heaven's name was I going to do with my life?

I went for the interview and accepted the position as a nursery school teacher in a private academy in Woodbury. I was to start the next week. Now I could afford to pay my room rent and buy gas for my car. I taught all day in the school. In the afternoon I got the courage to look for some clothes that I needed.

One day, I saw a three piece living room set for one hundred dollars that you put together yourself. I asked them to deliver it and now I had someplace in my room to sit. I had the eight hundred dollars that the publishing company gave me when I finished my book about religion and children. I decided to buy a little TV for myself. It gave me a warm feeling to work, come home to a house without nuns and their rules, eat supper, and watch TV upstairs in my room. This was such a change in my life and I loved it. Next, Mary's mother helped me apply for my own phone.

The arrangement for the room where I was living was this: I had to leave every Saturday and Sunday because her son and his wife would stay there. Thus every weekend I was homeless. Luckily I had the car. I drove around. Saturday was okay but the nights being homeless were scary. I would find a large hotel and sleep in the car in the parking lot. I could use their bathroom. As the weather got cold I figured I should get a good job in the public schools and find an apartment. A parent in the nursery school taught me how to apply for a teaching position. I did get a couple of offers from superintendents. They were much taken with my education and experience and were very interested in the fact that I had just left the convent. It was necessary to share this information with them, to explain the large gap in my employment experience.

Having taught for so many years in Bedford-Stuyvesant, I decided I would be very comfortable in an integrated area. I applied for a teaching job in the first grade of a Long Island school district and was accepted. The salary was a dream for me. I was to start in January. Now I could start looking for a place to live. There were several lovely garden apartments in town not far from the school. The friend I met in nursery school came with me to go apartment hunting. I found one that I loved. We went back to the real estate office. I put my entire paycheck down as security and rent.

I moved into a lovely garden apartment in a very nice town on Long Island. For furniture, I had a cot and an assemble-yourself couch. The next day the building superintendent rang my doorbell and told me that I could move my furniture into the apartment at anytime. People in that lovely building usually had large vans moving their furniture. When I told him I had already moved in, he could not believe his eyes—one cot and a couch. He just looked at me.

No one knew my background. The person who owned the apartment building said she could find no credit history on me. "I guess you pay everything with cash." I said "yes." I had my bachelor's degree in Business Administration but did not know about this credit history thing.

The Superintendent of the School District knew my background. I requested it be kept confidential. I did not want people staring at me. My principal was clued in for my sake, and he made sure to take care of me in circumstances that came up. He and his wife, Marge, became my dear friends. I was assigned to teach in a portable classroom in the schoolyard. This was great, for then I did not have to intermingle with other people. When I left on Friday, I said good-bye and did not speak to another person again until Monday morning. Food buying was tough on my budget. I had no money leftover the first month. Again, that is how I found myself going through those cartons at night behind the supermarket. I found apples, potatoes, and other vegetables discarded. It kept me going.

The nice lady that I met at the retreat house telephoned me and asked me to come to her ladies clothing store. She completely outfitted me, free of charge, with twelve outfits and a beautiful coat. God was certainly taking good care of me. All of the clothes she gave me were the best labels and very fashionable.

I usually did not go over to the main school building because I was shy. I did not want anyone to ask me questions about my former life. There was a rumor that I was divorced and hiding out from my husband. Several young people were teaching there. As the months went by, I began go to the main building. On one of those visits to the main building I met Diane and Ginny who became my lifelong friends.

The first time they asked me to meet them in the city at a singles bar on Second Avenue was a horror. Two of my friends moved over to the bar. A nice man was moving in on me, and I accepted it as friendly gesture. I was unknowingly allowing him to come on to me. After an hour he asked me to go outside with him. I said no. He said in a fierce loud voice that I wasted his time all night and I had some nerve. I stood there absolutely terrified he would hit me. My two friends ran over and took me out of there. I had told them of my background before this, so they realized now I had no experience with singles bars. I had so much to learn. Years later my friends and I laughed about that night.

Eileen visiting Las Vegas

26
The Single Scene

By the time winter arrived, my friends gave me a choice of going skiing or sitting alone in my apartment. They realized that I would probably like to hide from the world. I knew of the embarrassment that happens because I did not know how to act. Relax, they said, we will be there for you.

That is how I was introduced to the ski scene at Mount Snow in Vermont. It was here that I lost all of my inhibitions. I was an extrovert by nature, and now that part of my personality, which had been so stifled, was overflowing with good spirits and liveliness. I personally liked myself. I was enjoying life to the fullest.

We joined a ski house and went every other weekend. I did not know how to ski. There was a very nice guy named Andy who took the time to show me what clothes I needed, and even arranged a visit to the ski rental place so I could get fitted for boots, skis, and poles. Andy gave me a few lessons and suggested I join the ski school. Happy hour at the ski lodge after a day of skiing was the very best feeling. I sighed, realizing all that I had missed in life.

When we went out at night to the bars in Vermont, Andy would show me how to dance to attract attention. He told me never to accept a drink from a guy because he would expect me to stay by his side all night. "You have to make the rounds and enjoy people."

Andy was dating my friend Ginny. She was very happy with all he was doing to help her friend get acclimated to life in Vermont.

Skiing in Vermont, me on the left

One day, at the base of the mountain, a fellow skier asked me to go to the top of the mountain with him, and he would buy me lunch. I had never been up there and was really scared. He insisted. I thought to myself, *What the heck!* We went up in the gondola. Getting off at the top and moving away toward the top of the mountain, I nearly had a heart attack. I panicked. I could not move. He motioned to come on and follow him. I said to myself, *There is no way this is going to happen. I don't need a lunch that badly."* I sat down on my behind, held my poles, and slid all the way to the bottom. As skiers coasted by me, I must have been some sight to watch. When I arrived at the lodge door, he was nowhere to be found, and I never saw him again, thank God. I did not blame him.

27

Puerto Rico Vacation

Puerto Rico was offering a good deal in February. Kathy and I decided to go. I would have to take out a small loan to pay for it. We stayed at the San Juan Hotel. Our room was lovely. It was my first time on vacation. I had never seen a hotel room before in my life. We went down to the lounge area.

As we sat at the bar, Kathy met someone. I removed myself to give her privacy. There was a small table and two chairs by the entrance, inside the door. I sat there surveying this scene. I had so much to take in. I could handle this. The maître d' came over and told me he would send someone over. My eyes opened wide. I did not wish anyone, I told him. In a few minutes, a nice looking man joined me. I had no confidence. In any case, I had to be nice. He asked if I would like to go for a walk. I did not want to admit that I was scared and said yes to him. He was on a business trip and said perhaps I would enjoy seeing his room. Like a very simple person, I said, "Yes." It would be interesting to compare other rooms to ours. He must have wondered what planet I came from. Up we went, and as I entered his room he started to kiss me. He said, "Why won't you kiss me?" as he started to undress me. At that point I knew I was in a bad situation. It was my own doing. I opened the door and fled out of the room to the elevator. He ran after me wanting to know what was wrong. I said nothing. Later I learned that the table by the door was for prostitutes. I was trapped with my ignorance. For the rest of the trip I watched intently and tried to assimilate safely in this new environment.

28
Another Blind Date

A friend that I met in nursery school insisted that I meet her cousin. It seems that he was dedicating his life to assisting poor children. She thought it would be a good date for me. I was so tired of everyone trying to match me up with someone. I always said no. This time, I did not want to hurt her feelings. She was very kind to me. I agreed to have dinner at her home. Her cousin and her husband would be there. It was a pleasant meal.

The man's name was Gus. He shared with me all the awards that were given to him for his good works. While he was driving me home, Gus told me his life's work was to help the poor young boys of New York. He was not into dating at this time. I was very happy to hear that for I really did not want to go out with him. That solved that problem. This next part is hard to believe, but it did happen. A few weeks later as I was reading the paper, there was a picture of *Gus* on the front page. He had been arrested for transporting little boys across the border into Puerto Rico for purposes of sex. He ended up in jail. My friend could not find words to say how shocked she was to find this out about her cousin.

At this point I wrote to a friend of mine who was a religious brother. He liked me a lot. I suggested that he leave, and we could get married. I felt at this point that I needed someone to take care of me.

Then I would feel safe. He wouldn't leave for he had a big position in the church. Oh, well, it was a thought.

Abandoning that idea, I turned to new tactics. I had to be defensive. No more taking chances with my exciting life. Life goes on. There were numerous opportunities to explore in life. The relatively sheltered way of the convent was removed and at times left me feeling unprotected. On the other hand, I found my inner strength in relying on myself and being able to rest in the fact that I knew God was watching over me.

29
Meeting My Future Husband

The many circumstances that I found myself in have led me to believe that God is walking with us. In stepping out of my past life, I now was free to act as I choose. It has brought me to a good place on this Earth.

After a little while, I was introduced to my husband, John, on a blind date. On our second date he suggested that we go for a ride to Montauk Point. John had already packed a picnic lunch and a bottle of wine.

Going to Montauk on a date caused me to wonder about the circle of life. John did not know anything about the day I drove there a few years before, when I was trying to make a decision about leaving the convent. We went to the same spot on the cliff where I had been.

Years later we brought my young daughter to those same high cliffs to tell her the story. As we gazed out to the ocean, we wondered about it all.

Our daughter's medical school graduation

30
The Church

When we applied to get married in the church, we were told, "No." My husband was divorced, and I was an ex-nun. "What do you mean?" I asked the priest in the parish.

My anger was showing. After all that had gone on in the church, these few priests on the marriage council insisted on exerting their power to prevent us from marrying in the Catholic Church. So many times in the past I had dealt with this problem. This is why Sister Anna paid no attention to the rules. She had taught me to go around the rules and do good. I would follow her way. One holy priest told me to get married in a civil ceremony and then the council would probably agree to our ceremony in the church. It worked. We were married in a little white church on Long Island. The following wonderful reception included our families and friends. My family was in full attendance and cheerfully accepted the fact that I was not ever going to return to the convent.

I now look at myself and realize that God and Sister Anna were watching over me. Sister taught me well. I have been granted a rich love and a beautiful baby girl.

Epilogue

I now live in a little hamlet on Long Island with my husband, my daughter, and our little puppy. My dear parents and my beloved sister Margie have all passed on to heaven. I know they are now seeing through the eyes of God and understand completely why I left the convent. It is a soothing thought for my soul.

I get in my car and drive a short distance to the ocean. I walk in the sand along the beach, watching the waves crashing on the shoreline. The ripples they create remind me of my life: changing, charging, and slowly dancing back into the ocean to start again. Far out on the horizon, the sun glistens like rippling silk on the water, as though beckoning to me. I smile as I am reminded of Sister Anna, waving me on from her big leather chair, quietly accomplishing so much for the poor around us.

"At Sister Anna's Feet" is my personal story as I remember it and lived it. Perhaps those who are caring and working for the good of others, will see themselves in this story as they live in an ever changing world.

LOOK FOR THE

NEXT BOOK

MY LIFE AFTER THE CONVENT

COMING IN 2010

Printed in the United States
by Baker & Taylor Publisher Services